Evelyn Doyle now lives in Scotland with her partner, Michael. She trained as a psychiatric nurse, then became a police officer and later moved on to run her own company. She has one son, Benjamin, and a grandson, Joshua.

Evelyn

A True Story

EVELYN DOYLE

ORION

An Orion paperback

First published in Great Britain in 2002
by Orion Media
This paperback edition published in 2003
by Orion Books Ltd,
Orion House, 5 Upper St Martin's Lane,
London WC2H 9EA

A CIP catalogue record for this book is available
from the British Library.

Printed and bound in Great Britain by
Clays Ltd, St Ives plc

To my brothers, my best friends
with love

To loving fathers everywhere
separated from their children

'Quid dulsius hominum generi ab natura datum est
Quam sui cuique liberi'

'Of all nature's gifts to the human race
what is sweeter to a man than his children'

MARCUS TULLIUS CICERO

Acknowledgements

To the ladies of Fatima Mansions, especially 'Mrs Sullivan', thank you for caring.

To my 'Mothers' at High Park Convent, thank you for two happy years and allowing me to be a child.

My grateful thanks to Molly McCloskey for her editorial assistance.

For help with research

Tom Quinlan   National Archives of Ireland, Dublin

Des Mulhare   Four Courts Law Library, Dublin

Andrew Healey   Beattie and Healey Solicitors, Dublin

Regina Cogan   Irish Independent Newspaper, Dublin

Allison O'Reilly   ISPCC, Dublin

For love and support

To Michael, thank you darling, for your encouragement and support.

To my son Benjamin, for being my son, thank you, I love you so much.

I recognized her immediately. How could I not? She was, after all, my mother.

It was 1967 and I had made my way from Manchester to Glasgow to see her, for the first time in thirteen years. The journey seemed interminable and, as the train approached Glasgow, my nerves began to get the better of me. Fear, joy, and dread were doing battle. My travelling companions in the second-class compartment were three Church of England ministers. As I struggled not to cry, I prayed they wouldn't notice my distress. I needn't have worried; when I did cry, they ignored me.

As the train slowed, I considered for a moment not getting off. I gathered my belongings slowly and waited for the ministers to leave. I wanted to compose myself. My mind was full of questions. What would I say to her? Had I really forgiven her? Would I accept her explanation? Would she offer any? I was eight when my mother visited me in the industrial school, and that was the last time I'd seen her.

I stepped down onto a long dirty platform, disoriented by the throngs of people and the noise. Standing still, I searched the crowd until I spotted her. A small, slightly overweight, middle-aged woman. I knew it was her. She saw me too and waved tentatively. I waved back and walked towards her. We embraced, tightly, until I pulled away.

'Hello, how've you been?'

It was all I could think of to say. She told me she was fine and that she was so happy to have me back and that everything would be all right now.

'We must catch up on all the gossip,' she said.

The gossip? She sounded as though she'd met up with an old school pal. What kind of gossip did she mean? Did she want to talk about the latest fashion or pop records, or maybe she wanted to discuss the merits of matching lipstick and nail varnish?

'Do you smoke?' she asked.

I nodded. This was not how I imagined our meeting. She hailed a taxi. The cheerful driver put my bag on the floor and helped her into the cab.

'Where to, hen?'

I tried not to laugh; he hadn't said 'hen' to be funny. This was Glasgow, I reminded myself. She gave him the address and we filled his taxi with cigarette smoke and made small talk for the twenty-minute journey. The taxi pulled to a stop beside the garden gate of a fifties-style semi-detached council house. I noticed that the garden was a little untidy and the net curtains on the windows were not as white and crisp as those of her neighbours. She led me to the blue front door, but I saw her hesitate before she inserted the key into the brass lock. Beads of perspiration had appeared over her top lip.

'What's the matter?' I asked.

She looked as though she'd been about to say something but had changed her mind. She took a deep breath and opened the door.

'Mammy!'

A beautiful blue-eyed child of about five or six ran at my mother, who scooped her up and kissed her forehead.

'Who's that, Mammy?'

The child gazed at me over my mother's shoulder, her big eyes staring. She reminded me of someone but I couldn't think who. My mother lowered her to the ground and gave her a gentle pat.

'Where are the others?' my mother asked. 'Are they all in?'

I followed her into the living room. There were three other children scattered around the untidy room – a dark-haired boy of about thirteen, practically identical to one of my own brothers, a slightly plump but pretty girl of about twelve, and another boy who looked to be ten or eleven. They all swivelled round to stare at me. These children looked so familiar; the feeling of knowing them was strong. The older boy glared at me with what I imagined could only be hatred.

I smiled at them. I liked them immediately, and I wanted them to like me. No one had told me that my mother had another family, but I knew now. These children were my half-brothers and my half-sisters, and at once I felt glad that I had found my mother.

She started telling me their names. 'And this is my baby, Angela.'

She tickled the little one under her chin and the child squealed with delight. I was waiting for her to introduce me to the others – they would be thrilled as I was, wouldn't they? – then a man I recognized appeared from what must have been the kitchen and held out his hand to me.

'Hello, Gerry,' I said, shaking his hand.

Gerry was my father's first cousin. He was the man my mother had left with all those years ago.

Gerry looked uneasily at my mother. The muscles in my mother's jaw were working and her lips had become a thin hard line. Almost imperceptibly, she shook her head at him.

'How about a nice sup of tea?' she said to me.

She asked if I took sugar and then told Gerry to make the tea. He was headed towards the kitchen when her next words stopped him in his tracks.

'Children,' my mother said, 'this is Evelyn. I used to look after her when she was a little girl, while her mammy was in hospital.'

Gerry turned and stared at her. Anger contorted his soft features. Abruptly, he strode into the kitchen and slammed the door behind him.

The three youngest children smiled and said hello, but the older boy fixed his gaze on my mother, then left the room. My mother looked at me. I was her first-born child and this was the second time she had abandoned me.

Later when we were alone my Mother gave me her version of her marriage to my Father. It differed from my memories of those days that were not all that far back in time. Could this be her justification for abandoning us? I decided to find out. Over the years I talked to my father, but he didn't want to be reminded of what for him were dark days but he loved to talk about the happier times spent with his pals in his youth.

My search for the truth led me back to Fatima Mansions where I once again ate at Mrs Sullivan's table, and I couldn't imagine how I found ox heart and turnips delicious. I ate without complaint, something told me she still had that old slipper in her apron pocket.

Mr Beattie was living in splendid retirement out in Sandy Cove overlooking Dublin Bay and was childishly delighted to have been part of our story.

My Father is dead now, but this is his story, it is my story; but more than anything it is a story of courage and love, a unique love that can only exist between Father and Daughter.

ONE

1953 started as it meant to go on. Daddy was in hospital. We didn't know yet what was wrong with him. We were scared he would die, and we said special prayers for him at bedtime. One day I went to the chapel on my way home from school. I didn't have a penny to light a candle for Daddy but I told God that when I was rich I'd pay Him back, and I lit the biggest candle I could find. I didn't linger. Someone might have come and noticed the big candle and known it was me. I tiptoed to the door and slunk out, happy in the knowledge that Daddy would get better soon.

I ran as fast as I could down Basin Street and in no time reached the iron bridge over the canal. The steps were slippy but I didn't falter. I had crossed this bridge every day for the last couple of years. Our flats, Fatima Mansions, were on the far side of the canal. The flats had been built by the government at the start of the 1950s, when they were trying to house all the people who'd been living in the slums of Dublin. Fatima Mansions consisted of several grey concrete four-storey blocks of flats, with concrete balconies running along each storey. The blocks were lettered A to K; our flat was on the first landing of J block.

Some of the boys from our block were fishing from the bank, and I stopped to watch. A shout went up.

'Jaysus, will you look at that!'

It was Mickey Sullivan. He pointed up the canal. All eyes looked in that direction and the boys started running towards what Mickey was pointing at. A large dead pig was floating on its side towards us, its pink body swollen and its short thick legs sticking straight out. I could see one wide-open blue eye. It stared straight at me as it passed under the iron bridge. I blessed myself and bolted back over the bridge to the chapel. I rushed in and blew out the candle. An old lady on her knees looked at me in fury, then shook her fist.

'Ye young rip, ye! God forgive ye.'

I hoped He would. I would confess before I made my First Holy Communion in May, and I wouldn't see any more dead bodies.

Daddy had been in hospital for a long time. We found out he had lead poisoning. It came from the paints he used at work. I didn't think God was hearing our prayers. Mammy had been out a lot since Daddy'd gone to hospital. Mrs Sullivan, who lived next door, said Mammy ought to be ashamed of herself, leaving the babbies on their own.

'She should be looking after her children,' she said to Mrs Moore.

The two women leaned on the balcony wall, watching their children play on the street below.

'Ah now Mrs Sullivan, where she goes is a mystery, I swear to God.'

Mrs Moore blessed herself, then pulled a packet of Sweet Aftons from her grubby apron pocket and offered one to Mrs Sullivan. They puffed contentedly in silence for a moment.

'And poor Dessie lying on his back in hospital,' Mrs Sullivan continued. 'They say he's got the lead poisoning.' They both blessed themselves at the mention of the hospital.

'Anyway, I'm not one for gossiping. Now, I'd better be after making Joe his dinner.'

Mrs Sullivan nipped out her cigarette and put the butt in her apron pocket. She had thirteen children of her own. All the kids in our block of flats had a healthy respect for her and for the old slipper she kept in her apron. Although she was a large woman with big knots of varicose veins running up her legs, she had no trouble catching us if we tried to run away. But Mrs Sullivan was also the first person you'd go to if you were in trouble. Her daughter Angela was my best friend and sometimes I sneaked in with her for a bit of tea. The Sullivans' flat was warm and clean and there were always nice cooking smells coming from it. If Mrs Sullivan had ever bothered to take a head count, she'd have realised she was feeding at least four extra mouths.

She saw me sitting on the top step of the landing. She wasn't concerned that I had heard what she'd said about my mammy; she'd said it often enough to her face. Mammy used to cry when Mrs Sullivan gave out to her. She said Mrs Sullivan didn't know what it was like for her.

'All right so,' Mrs Sullivan would say, 'Joe works, but it's only at Jacob's Biscuit factory. He doesn't earn as much as your Dessie and him a tradesman as well. So think about that!'

After Mrs Sullivan left, Mammy would call her 'a feckin interfering bitch' and have a go at one of the boys in a temper. She wouldn't do this to me; I'd have told Daddy and then there would have been holy war.

The flat was getting dark. I had no sixpence for the meter and I hoped Mammy would come home soon. The gas stove was working and I boiled some water. My brothers arrived back. There were six of us in all, and I was the oldest and the only girl. I was seven and just after me was Noel, who was six. Maurice and John were five and four, and the babies, Kevin and Dermot, were three and one.

The boys hadn't been to school that day. It was Maurice's turn to look after the two babies and he'd been wheeling them around in the big old pram. Maurice told me he'd robbed some biscuits from a shop on the other side of Fatima Mansions and hadn't been caught. He was pleased with himself for being able to feed the babies.

'I'll do an Act of Contradiction when I've done my Hail Marys for Daddy.'

I poured warm water from the black kettle onto tea leaves in jam jars, but it looked weak and nobody drank it. At last Mammy came home. Her eyes were red, as if she'd been crying. She seemed to be in a temper again and it didn't get any better when I told her there was no money for the meter. She made me go next door to Mrs Sullivan and ask for the lend of a shilling. I hated asking for money, but I went anyway because I didn't want her to send me to the pawnshop.

Mrs Sullivan had no money to spare, but she said she did have some ribs and cabbage left over and would bring them along shortly. I decided to go and wait outside the back of Mr Hennessey's shop to see if he had any empty tea or currant chests. Mr Gleason over in K block paid three pence each for them if they were good enough, though we had no idea what he did with them. When I was nearly at the shop, Noel and Maurice found me.

'You'd better come back,' they said, 'Mammy's in a real temper!'

I told them to wait with me to see if we could get some chests. When Mr Hennessey came out with his rubbish, I asked him. I liked Mr Hennessey. He always smiled and sometimes he would give us a Cleaves toffee when Mammy paid her bill on Friday. He looked at us and rubbed his chin. He always rubbed his chin when he was thinking. Now his eyes were crinkled just as when he smiled.

'Well, you know it's Wednesday and I don't usually empty the tea and currants until Friday.'

We all looked at him without saying anything. He seemed to take a long time to make up his mind. At last he told us to wait a minute and went into his shop. We couldn't see into the back of the shop but we heard Mr Hennessey bumping into things and grunting and saying prayers. We couldn't think why he'd be saying prayers.

Finally, he came out the back door, dragging three currant chests and one tea chest behind him. This was treasure indeed! We could get loads of currants at the bottom and in the side cracks and Mammy could make a pudding. I asked him for a paper bag. He made a clicking noise with his tongue and took a big breath, but I knew he wasn't cross with me. He handed me a big brown paper bag with three Cleaves toffees inside.

'Oh, thank you, Mr Hennessey.'

I gave one to Noel and one to Maurice and put the other

in my mouth, but I had to spit it out into my hand to thank Mr Hennessey again.

'Now feck off out of my sight,' he said.

He half smiled at us and disappeared through the back door of the shop. The door shut with a bang and we heard Mr Hennessey saying more prayers.

We each took a currant chest and started scraping the currants out of them and putting them in the bag Mr Hennessey had given us. Maurice was too small to reach to the bottom of his chest and he turned it on its side so he could crawl in. I told him not to be eating them. We wanted Mammy to be pleased with us, so we had to get as many currants as we could.

We dragged the chests through the streets of the flats until we reached K block. My brothers waited at the bottom of the stairs while I went up to see if Mr Gleason was in. There were other people who bought the chests but Mr Gleason was the nearest. I said a Hail Mary on my way because he frightened me to death. Mr Gleason was what Daddy called a dirty oul gurrier. His face was a deep purple and had scars and pockmarks, and his nose was like a potato gone off. The stink of his greasy coat was terrible, and I didn't like the way he always tried to get me into his flat. He lived on the top landing. I was out of breath when I reached his door.

'Come in out of that cold, pet,' he said.

He smiled, showing that he had only one or two dark brown stumps for teeth. The smell that came from the flat nearly made me sick. It was worse than the smell of the ferret Daddy kept in the coal hole for when he went rabbiting, worse even than the smell that came from the canal sometimes in summer. I didn't want to go in. I told him that my brothers were waiting at the bottom of the stairs and I was in a hurry for my tea. I didn't tell him that if he didn't buy the chests, there'd be no tea tonight.

He coughed for a long time. His face went an even deeper purple and awful noises came from somewhere in his chest. I stood back as far as I could without actually climbing on the balcony wall. He spat out a big gob of green slime that almost landed on my shoe. I wanted to be sick again, but I remembered why I was there.

'I've got three currant chests and a tea chest, Mr Gleason. My brothers are minding them down at the bottom. They're very good, honest!'

I waited for him to finish coughing. I tried not to look, and I knew it would be impolite to stick my fingers in my ears, so I sang a song in my head to shut out the sound. But I could still hear Mr Gleason's cough.

'Well,' he said, 'bring them up and I'll have a look.'

His voice had squeaks and whistles in it. I leaned over the balcony and shouted down to my brothers to bring the chests up.

Noel shouted back and said, 'Do you think we're feckin donkeys or what?'

I could hear them dragging the chests up the concrete stairs, and I bolted down. If they were damaged, we'd get less for them. We finally got the four wooden chests lined up against the balcony wall for Mr Gleason's inspection. He gave nothing away as he looked at them.

'I'll give you tuppence each for them,' he said, 'they're not as good as they should be.'

I had banked on getting three pence, and I told him so.

'Mr Devlin at the farmyard will give me three pence,' I said. 'They're brand new. Mr Hennessey has just emptied them. They're worth three pence.'

I was almost crying. It was getting dark now and we wouldn't have time to go to Mr Devlin. The farmyard was way over at the other side of the flats. Mr Gleason was coughing and he spat again. I wanted to get away from him. I told Noel and Maurice to pick up the chests.

'All right, you young rip,' Mr Gleason said, 'three pence it is.'

He went into his flat and came out with a shilling. I held this treasure tightly in my hand, and the three of us charged down the stairs and out onto the street.

As we walked back towards our block, I told the boys that tomorrow we were going to see Daddy in the hospital. We knew the hospital was on Cork Street because we walked past it when we went for free dinners at the Vincent de Paul. I didn't like their dinners. They boiled the potatoes in their skins and served them with black pudding and cabbage. Sometimes Mammy had a few pennies, and we would go to the cake shop on the way home and get a Vienna loaf and a cream cookie, but Mammy hadn't taken us anywhere since Daddy had been in hospital.

I decided to tell Mammy that we only got sixpence and to use the rest to get something for Daddy. 'We're going to buy Daddy an Easter egg,' I told the boys, 'for when we see him tomorrow.'

I trusted my brothers not to let on about the shilling. We stopped at Mr Hennessey's shop to change it. I asked his sour-faced oul one for one sixpence and two threepenny bits. She started to say something and Mr Hennessey gave her a stern look. She got bad tempered but changed the shilling anyway. I put a threepenny bit in each of my socks, and hoped Mammy wouldn't find them.

The next day, I waited for Mammy to go out. She wasn't in a hurry but I knew it wouldn't be long before she went.

'Mind the babbies and see if Mrs Sullivan can give you a bit of dinner. I won't be long.'

And she left. I didn't feel sad that day like I usually did when she went out. That day, we were going to see Daddy. I put the three youngest boys in the 'carriage'. Noel and I pushed it and Maurice held the handle. The wheels were bockety and it was hard to push. Daddy had bought the pram when I was born. The man in the swanky shop in Grafton Street had told him they had cheaper ones, but Daddy's mind was made up: this was the one for his new daughter and nothing else would do. The man told Daddy that the 'carriage', as he called it, was fifteen guineas and a further one guinea for delivery. That was more than a month's wages. Daddy gave the man one pound and ten shillings deposit and went to see Granddad. They both went back to the shop and paid for the pram, much to the surprise of the snooty man.

We got to Dolphin's Barn. People were cursing at us, but we couldn't help bumping into them on the busy paths. The pram wouldn't go exactly where we wanted it to. A horse drawing a pigswill cart had to pull up suddenly as we pushed the pram across to the other side of the road. We bought Daddy a chocolate marshmallow Easter egg from a little shop that smelled of tobacco and lavender. The man in the shop let us spend ages choosing the right egg for Daddy. We settled on one in glittery red and silver paper.

We took turns carrying it. Some of the paper came off and we each took a small flake of chocolate. Daddy wouldn't notice, we were sure. When we reached the big iron gates of Coombe Hospital, we saw a man in a small hut just inside the gate. His suit had shiny buttons on it. Noel and Maurice tried to push the gate open, but it was too heavy, and I couldn't let go of the pram because the brake wasn't working. The man came to the gate. We told him that we wanted to see our daddy. He walked out onto the path and tickled the baby under his chin. Dermot laughed and tried to grab one of the shiny buttons on the man's coat.

'They don't let children in to visit,' the man said. 'I'm sorry.'

I got in an awful temper. I told the man that we hadn't seen Daddy for a long time. Anyway, I said, we had bought him an Easter egg and even though it was mostly just marshmallow now, we had to give Daddy his present because it would help him to get better. I stared at the man and said again that we had to see our daddy.

The man bent down on one knee and, holding my arms, he said, 'I'll tell you what. I'll get your Easter egg to your daddy for you. What's his name?'

Noel and Maurice looked at me with the same funny face. We had just told the man his name.

'His name is Daddy!' they shouted. I knew we were Doyles, but didn't say anything.

I gave the man the Easter egg. He said that he would find our daddy and tell him we had called to see him. He patted my head and put a shilling in my hand and I reminded myself to say a Hail Mary for this nice man.

'Get off with you now,' he said, as he went back inside the gate.

On our way back to Dolphin's Barn, we bought chips wrapped in newspaper and hurried to the flat as fast as the bockety wheels on the pram would let us. Noel tore a piece of lino off the floor from a dark corner of the room and we lit a fire in the grate. We all sat on the floor and ate the chips by a blazing fire. We were happy and full; we were even warm. It was a good day. We stayed where we were, singing songs that Daddy sometimes sang to us. Our favourite was

> *Whenever you go to Kilkenny*
> *Look out for the hole in the wall*
> *Twenty-four eggs for a penny*
> *And butter for nothing at all*

Noel told us a joke that a big boy at school had told him.

'Paddy Englishman, Paddy Scotsman and Paddy Irishman went up in an airplane. The plane was going to crash and there were only two parachutes. Paddy Scotsman and Paddy Irishman got the parachutes and went to jump. Paddy Englishman shouted, "What am I to do?" Paddy Irishman shouted on his way down, "Put butter on your arse and slide down the rainbow."'

We laughed till the tears ran down our faces. We thought 'arse' was the funniest word we'd ever heard. Mammy came home and found us rolling around on the floor, making a terrible noise with our laughter, but we couldn't tell her what we were laughing at.

*

Daddy was coming home. Mammy had cleaned the flat and Mrs Sullivan had given her a lend of some sheets and blankets. Granny had been to visit and made stew and some custard to go with the apple pies Mammy had baked. I stood beside the table and ate the skins of the apples as they fell in a long curl off the fruit. They gave me an awful bellyache, but I wished it could be like this all the time. I loved the cooking smells and the clean sheets on the bed. I loved my hair washed and soft and tied up with a green ribbon, and I liked the smell of soap on the babies. I liked being able to go to school every day. What I liked best of all, though, was not having to go to Mr Gleason.

When Daddy came home he looked awful white and his bones were sticking out. It made me cry. I was afraid to sit on his knee in case I hurt him. He told me that the food in the hospital was worse than pigswill.

'But now I'm home,' he said, 'and Mammy will soon fatten me up. Sure haven't I to go back to work soon?'

He held up his skinny arms and my brothers sang to him:

> Skinny malink melodeon egg an umbrella free
> Went to the pictures and couldn't get a seat
> When the picture started
> Skinny malink farted
> Skinny malink melodeon egg an umbrella free

We all laughed. Daddy told the boys he would box their ears, but he laughed too; even Mammy laughed.

After a few weeks at home, Daddy began to get annoyed

easily and he spent a lot of time in his special room. He played the piano very loud and Mrs Sullivan banged on the wall and shouted, 'Holy Mother of God, Dessie, will you give us some peace?'

Daddy banged back and played even louder. When Granddad visited he brought his cello and they played most of the day. They loved marching music and very old songs. Mrs Sullivan called Daddy a 'feckin bowsie' and told him she would call the Gardai.

Finally, Daddy got work painting down in the country. He would be away for six weeks. My heart sank. Over the last few weeks Mammy had not gone out during the day and the flat was clean and tidy. There was a smell of cooking when I came home from school. Daddy combed my hair and put plaits in it every morning, and he always found some pretty ribbons to tie in a bow at the end of my plaits.

One day at school, we were in art class making models and a girl named Chrissie Kernan had pulled my ribbons out so that my plaits came undone. In the models, we were using plastic bits that looked like large orange pips and I was so annoyed with Chrissie that I stuffed some of the pips in her ear. The next day Chrissie and her mother burst into the classroom, her mother shouting at the nun to tell her which 'rip' had caused her daughter the pain in the ear.

'I'll box her fecking ears! Pardon my Irish, Sister.' She blessed herself.

Chrissie was holding a cloth to her ear and her cheek was red and swollen. She snuffled and wiped her runny nose with the back of her sleeve. The nun held up her hand to silence the woman.

'All right, Mrs Kernan,' she said, 'we'll get the child responsible for this.'

The class went very quiet; we were all waiting to see what would happen next. This was better than doing sums or the catechism. I had a lump in my chest, though. If I had caused Chrissie's face to look like that, I was surely in trouble. I decided to own up. As I stood up, my chair made a terrible noise on the wooden floor and everyone turned to look at me.

'She pulled my plaits out and I lost my ribbon!'

I thought the nun might have considered that a good enough reason to stuff Chrissie's ear full of pips, but I was wrong. She came over to my desk and pulled me to the front of the class. Mrs Kernan gave me a black look. I wanted to stick my tongue out at her but I knew this was not the time. The nun dragged me by the sleeve of my cardigan along the corridor to the Mother Superior's office. Chrissie and her mother came too, Mrs Kernan gabbing the whole way about young ones today. The Mother Superior told Mrs Kernan to take Chrissie to the hospital while she dealt with me.

The school sent for my Mammy, who wasn't at all pleased to be lectured by the Mother Superior on how to turn me into a 'nice young lady'. I was sent home with Mammy. As she dragged me through the streets, she shouted at me and slapped me around the ears, and I screamed more in shame than pain. When we finally got to the flat, Daddy said he thought I'd been punished enough. I promised never to stuff anything into anyone's ears again and, when I went to Mr Hennessey's to get Daddy his twenty Gold Flake, he gave me a penny to spend on sweets.

I watched as Daddy got ready to go. He poured sugar and tea into little knots of brown paper and placed them along with his billycan into a canvas bag. In a small brown case, he packed his white overalls and his special shoes for inside. He told me that some of these houses had cream-coloured carpets you could get lost in. I had a lump in my chest. I didn't want him to go away, but he said that he would come home every couple of weeks for a day or so.

'So you be a good girl now,' he said, 'and help your mammy with the babies. I might even bring you a nice present.'

He hugged us all at the bottom of the stairs and got into his black Austin and started to drive away. My brothers and several boys from our block ran after him, trying to race the car out onto the main street. Daddy tooted the horn and was gone.

The next day Mammy went out and left me to look after the babies. She went out nearly every day after that. I had to go to Mr Hennessey's for tea and currant chests again. One day the rain was lashing down when I went for the chests. I only got one and I was in bad humour. When I got back to the flat, I saw that one of the babies was missing.

'Where's Kevin?' I said.

It seemed that no one had seen him for a while. I lit the gas stove and put the blackened kettle on to boil. Kevin was nearly three and I was afraid he'd found his way out onto the main road.

'Look after the others,' I said to Noel and Maurice. 'I'm going to find Kevin.'

I kept my wet coat on and headed down the stairs. I started running towards where the flats ended and as I got near C block I saw something splashing about in a large puddle. Water was overflowing up onto the street through one of the gratings and there was Kevin, sitting in the middle of this dirty water and playing, just as though he were at Dollymount Strand. I dragged him out and carried this soggy bundle to the flat, while he screamed to be let back to his puddle.

As I reached the top stair of our landing, Mrs Sullivan came charging towards me. She grabbed my coat and whipped it off and quickly wrapped something in it.

'Tell your mammy I'm at the hospital with the babbie!' And she was off.

Inside the flat, I found all my brothers bawling. I could smell something burning. There were bits of half burnt rags and burned papers scattered about the place and the pram was full of water. No one could tell me what had happened, but I noticed that Dermot, who was only a year, wasn't there.

'Oh, Holy Mother!'

It was Dermot that Mrs Sullivan had wrapped in my coat.

My mother came home to find the flat full of screaming kids, angry women from the flats and a garda. Her face went white. The garda asked Mrs Moore if she would ever take the children out for a few minutes. Mrs Moore was delighted to be involved and she gathered up the two youngest boys. Before she went out, she looked at Mammy and hissed, 'God forgive ye!' And she blessed herself.

Mammy was shouting, 'For Christ's sake, will someone tell me what's going on?'

She told all the women to 'feck off out of her house'. Mrs Sullivan grabbed her arm and pulled her into the bedroom. I could hear her giving out to Mammy. Then I heard Mammy let out a blood-curdling scream and she ran back into the living room. She was trying to make for the hall door but the garda pulled her back. I ran to her and she held me tight. I had my arms around her waist; it was strange, I wanted to protect her. I knew this was serious. The baby had been badly burned in his pram. The garda told all the women to leave the flat because he wanted to speak to the mother in private. Mrs Sullivan took Noel and Maurice by the hand.

'I'll give them a bit of tea,' she said, and turned to me. 'Do you want something to eat, pet?'

I shook my head; I wanted to stay with Mammy. I thought I was in trouble with the garda because I had been told to mind the babies. I wanted to be sick. The lump in my chest was there again, and I started to cry.

'We'll send for your husband, Mrs Doyle,' the garda said. 'He's responsible for the welfare of his children and I'll have to get Mr Wogan from the NSPCC involved as well.'

Mammy got very upset and pleaded with the garda. 'Surely you don't have to disturb Dessie at work?' Daddy wasn't due to come home for two more weeks and she knew that this would put him in a terrible temper.

'Do you want to go to the hospital and see the baby?' the garda asked. 'I'll take you there myself and we can talk on the way.'

After they left, I went to Mrs Moore's. She was frying sausages.

'Give me a hand, Evelyn. Here, do some cuts of bread.'

I started to cut the long batch loaf into thick slices. The sausages smelt delicious and I remembered how hungry I was. Mrs Moore was giving out about my mother leaving us alone and talking about what Daddy would do when he came back. She seemed to be enjoying Mammy's trouble. I tried not to listen. I was desperate to know how bad Dermot was, but she wouldn't tell me. I moved over beside her at the gas stove. The cigarette dangling from her mouth had a long roll of ash on it that I was sure would drop into the sausages, but it hung there by some miracle and didn't fall even when she spoke. When I saw her flip the sausages with her long dirty fingernails, I felt sick and forgot that I was hungry.

'Will my brothers be all right here for a while?' I asked. 'I want to go and see Noel and Maurice at Mrs Sullivan's.'

I left without waiting for an answer and went along the balcony to Mrs Sullivan and her warm clean home.

It was night-time when Mammy came back from the hospital. Her eyes were red and had dark rings under them. She asked Mrs Sullivan to mind the boys for a little while longer. She wanted to speak to me alone.

'Dermot is very sick,' she said, and started to cry.

I stood and looked at her without saying anything. It was my fault and I was sure I would have to go to the magdalen's. They were laundries where they sent girls who were wayward or criminals or got pregnant before they were married. Mammy pulled me onto her lap and hugged me. I started to shake with fear; I was so frightened I couldn't even cry. Mammy stopped crying and stood me up in front of her, holding both my arms and forcing me to look straight at her.

'Listen carefully,' she said. She was very serious, which only frightened me more. 'The Gardai have sent for your daddy. You have to tell him that I was hanging out the washing when Dermot got burned. Do you hear me?'

She shook me hard; her fingers were hurting my arms. I tried to wriggle away but I couldn't.

'But Mammy,' I heard myself saying, 'it's been raining all day. I can't tell him you were hanging out the wash.'

She got very cross then. She stamped around the room, smoking a cigarette, and I followed her with my eyes. She was muttering to herself, but I couldn't make out what she was saying. I was desperate to know how Dermot was.

'Very bad!' she shouted. 'And if you'd been looking after him like I told you he wouldn't be where he is now!'

I ran out of the flat and made my way to the end of the road where there was a grotto dedicated to Our Lady of Fatima. I knelt down in the rain and begged the Holy Mother not to let Dermot die and not to let the Gardai send me to the magdalen's, and I promised never to steal another candle from the chapel. I looked at the perfect face of the statue and tried to find some comfort in it, but I couldn't. I made my way to the playing field. The gates were locked, but I climbed the railing and sat on the top, thinking what I could do to make Dermot better. Finally, I got the courage to go home and was happy to see that my Granny had come over from Dún Laoghaire. She was wearing her flowery apron and smelled of lavender. She hugged me to her and I started to cry again.

'I had to look for Kevin,' I said. 'I didn't burn the baby. Don't let them send me to the magdalen's. Please, Granny, please take me to live with you at the seaside!'

Granny looked angrily at Mammy while she held me close. She led me to the bathroom and insisted I have a hot bath. She'd put money in the meter and was busy cleaning the flat. I felt better after my bath, and Granny gave me something to eat and saw me off to bed. I shared the big bed with four of my brothers. That night, Granny made us join her when she said a whole rosary for Dermot.

Lying awake in bed the next morning, I heard the familiar sound of Daddy's car pulling up outside the flats. I turned to the boys and shouted, 'Daddy's home!'

All the boys woke up. Still sitting in bed, we broke into our usual song for such occasions.

Clap hands clap hands till Daddy comes home
With cakes in his pockets for us alone!

I heard my mother outside in the hallway cry out, 'Jaysus!'

Then we remembered poor Dermot and didn't feel so happy anymore. We raced to get dressed and Noel and Maurice got tangled up, with one leg each in the same pair of shorts. They fell and Noel shouted at Maurice, 'You've got my shorts on!'

After they'd straightened themselves out, we rushed out of the bedroom and headed straight for the big chair in the corner of the living room.

When Daddy came in, he was like a demon. I ran to him and he gave me a quick hug, then held my head between his hands and sat down. He looked as if he was speaking but there was no sound coming out. He got redder and redder until he exploded and began to bellow at Mammy. The boys and I sat very quietly, huddled in the big old armchair. I didn't understand some of the words Daddy said but they made Mammy cry.

'And what about Evelyn?' he shouted. 'Any other man would give you the hiding you deserve.'

He paused to wipe the spit from his mouth, then continued yelling. I had never seen him in a temper like this before. I put my hands to my ears to shut out the noise. The boys started crying and then everyone was screaming. I looked at Mammy sobbing and I cried louder. The boys screamed harder and very soon Daddy covered his ears too. Then Daddy stopped shouting. Our screaming died down to whimpering. Finally, there was silence. Mammy and Daddy went into the bedroom and closed the door and began shouting at each other again.

There was a knock at the front door. Daddy told me to answer it and tell whoever it was to feck off. I opened the door and saw a plump man with a peaked hat and a dark green uniform. Beside him was a woman with ginger hair. She wore a long blue cloak fastened at the front with two red straps and carried a bag just as the doctor did when he came with new babies. I thought maybe she had brought us a baby sister.

The man said, 'Hello, Evelyn. I'm Inspector Wogan. Is your daddy in?'

He must have known Daddy was in because the whole block could hear him shouting. Thinking he was a garda, I slammed the door shut and ran to the bedroom to tell

Daddy. Daddy had a wild look on his face. He told me to sit with my brothers and he went to the door. In a normal voice, he invited the man in. The man and the ginger-haired woman followed Daddy into the living room. She took off her cloak and laid it over the back of the chair. Her arms and face were covered in big red freckles. She looked strange to me. She held out her hand and led me into our bedroom. I was afraid to go but Daddy said it would be all right.

In the bedroom she told me to take off my clothes. I was horrified, but did as she asked. She inspected me all over and when she looked behind my ears it hurt because of the sores. She lifted up my hair and ran her fingers through it, smiling at me the whole time. When she'd finished her inspection, she told me I would have to go to Bride Road for a special bath. Then she led me back to the living room and took all my brothers into the bedroom together. Daddy and the man were talking.

Daddy said, 'I want her prosecuted. It's only a miracle the babies are not dead.'

I trembled and tried to make myself as small as I could in the armchair.

Inspector Wogan hunched his shoulders, spread out his arms, and turned his palms towards heaven. 'I understand completely, Mr Doyle,' he said, 'but as head of the family you are responsible and you are the one I would have to prosecute. And that wouldn't help anybody at all now, would it?'

Daddy paced back and forth, taking long draws on his cigarette. He was snorting the smoke out of his nostrils. It reminded me of a dragon in one of my schoolbooks and I tried not to laugh. The nurse brought the boys back into the living room. She told Mr Wogan that we all needed to go to Bride Road Baths for delousing, and she said that I was infested with impetigo.

I looked at the floor and hung my head. I felt ashamed and responsible. Mammy was in the bedroom all this time and never came out. Daddy led Mr Wogan and the woman to the door and I heard him agree to take us all to the baths at nine o'clock the next morning. When they were gone, Daddy went into the bedroom and shouted more at Mammy. Noel and Maurice thought it was great to be lousy and left the flat to tell all their friends the news.

The next day we all piled into Daddy's car, all except for Mammy. She stayed home. Daddy drove through the streets and pulled up outside a big red building. As we were getting out of the car, he muttered to himself, 'The disgrace of it,' he cursed.

I blessed myself and prayed that Daddy wouldn't go to purgatory for swearing about Mammy in the street.

Inside, a fat nurse wearing a stiff white apron walked towards us. Her uniform made a scratchy sound as she moved. John and Kevin hid behind Daddy's legs. Noel and Maurice and I huddled together. The nurse told Daddy to follow her, and her voice boomed under the high ceilings. A younger nurse with a kind face came in and took me away.

Daddy said, 'It's all right, pet. Don't be frightened. I'll wait right here for you.'

I started crying. This was the magdalen's for sure, I thought, as I followed the nurse down the corridor. There were black and white tiles on the floor and green ones on the walls and everything echoed. I stopped crying and said a few words out loud just to hear the echo and I stamped my feet as we walked. We entered a very long room with a row of big white baths standing on feet that looked like animals' claws. Beside each bath, there was a green canvas screen hung from a white metal frame on wheels. The nurse pulled one of the frames over so we couldn't be seen and began filling the bath with water. She told me to undress. Twice now in two days I'd had to take my clothes off in front of strangers. The tiles were cold on my bare feet and I tried to cover up my naked body with my hands and arms while the nurse went to a cupboard and brought out the biggest bottle I had ever seen. It was filled with a pale pink liquid, which she poured into the bath water.

'Hop in,' she said.

I stood on one leg and thought to myself: I'm not going to make it, the bath is too high. I jumped into the air and missed the bath, landing on my bum and letting out a yell that bounced round the room. The nurse smiled kindly.

'Goodness, child, have you never been in a bath before? Put one leg in and pull the other one behind you and before you know it your whole self will be in the bath.'

I did as she said. The water felt thick and warm like jelly and it made me think of a pudding we sometimes ate. I leaped straight back out but the nurse told me not to be a silly girl. She said that I was to stay in for 15 minutes.

'You even have to put your head under for a minute. That way you'll get rid of all those nasty sores on your poor body.'

The water was just beginning to go cold when she told

me I could get out. She handed me a pile of clothes that weren't mine. They were all brand new and, as I put them on, I felt overjoyed. I didn't often get new clothes. I walked with the nurse back to Daddy and saw that my brothers were wearing new clothes too. We all laughed out loud, except for Daddy. He looked cross, but I knew it wasn't with us.

Daddy didn't go away from home to work again. He got a job instead painting some houses in Dublin. Mammy didn't go out during the day after that either. And I didn't have to go to Mr Hennessey for tea and currant chests.

One day, Daddy's picture was in the newspaper. He had the job of painting all the bus stops in Dublin and I pretended to my friends that he was a famous film star, being in the paper like that. He was holding a paint pot in one hand and a little wooden ladder under his arm. He was wearing his white overalls and had a huge smile on his face. The women in the block said he looked like Nelson Eddie. Mammy said she wished he earned as much money as Nelson Eddie.

I still hadn't been able to see Dermot in hospital. But life was getting back to normal. Daddy and Mammy went to see Dermot every day. I was desperate for him to get better. I said many prayers and even managed to light a couple of candles for him in the chapel. One of the nuns at my school gave me a holy medal to put on Dermot's cot. The medal had been blessed by Pope Pius XII himself. I threaded one of Daddy's shoelaces through it and tied it round my neck for safekeeping.

One day Mammy gave me tuppence to go to the farm

for a dozen eggs so that she could make the Christmas pudding. Mary Flynn, who lived in the flat under us, said she would come along because she wanted to take her dog for a walk. Rex was a ginger-coloured mongrel. Mary used to boast that he was a pure bred, but she never said a pure bred what.

We walked down to the canal and across the busy street that had the grand houses on the other side of it. Rex was excited to be out and kept pulling Mary along. She was swearing at him and beating him on the head with the chain lead. I told her a few times to stop hitting him but she gave Rex an awful whack right on the side of his mouth. He howled in pain. I bent down to put my arms around his neck, to make him feel better.

The next thing I heard was Mary screaming. My head bumped on the path and Rex was standing over me, growling, his teeth bared. A big boot flashed past my head, and Rex was sent flying, howling as he went. When I looked up, there was a crowd of grown-ups gathered around me.

A garda was shouting, 'Get out of it! Get out of it!' He knelt down and looked at me and said, 'Holy Mother of Christ, where's the feckin dog?'

A man was holding Rex by the chain.

Mary Flynn was screaming, 'He didn't do it, he didn't do it! Give me back my dog!'

I looked at Rex, who was frightened out of his wits. His eyes were bulging and he could hardly breathe. The garda put his fingers in the dog's mouth and took something out. Then he dug a hanky out of his trouser pocket and shook it loose, placing whatever it was he'd got from Rex's mouth into the hanky. Something warm, sticky and wet was running down my neck and into my hair. I couldn't move and I didn't feel anything. A lady from one of the grand houses was running towards me. She had the whitest, fluffiest towel I had ever seen and she knelt down beside me and held it to my face.

The garda was speaking to the driver of a van that he'd stopped. I heard him say, 'I don't feckin care what you have to do, you're taking this child to the hospital.'

I saw that the lady's towel was turning red and I was afraid that the lovely fluffy thing would be destroyed. The lady told me not to worry; the towel was mine to keep, she said, she had plenty more. The garda lifted me into the back of the van. I could smell raw meat and it was cold. I fell asleep.

When I woke, I heard the garda saying, 'Honest, Mrs Doyle, I really do have your daughter in the back of the van and she's badly hurt. You'd better hurry.'

Mammy looked in the back of the van and said, 'Oh my God, what will Dessie say?'

She fainted and fell into the arms of the garda, and he put her in the van beside me. I thought she was dead. When Mammy woke up, she started to cry. She was holding my head now and my face was beginning to ache. Whenever we went round a corner, we slid all over the back of the van. We pulled up outside Coombe Hospital, the same place Daddy'd been when he had lead poisoning, and the garda carried me inside. I was taken into a room and a lady doctor came to see me. She told me she was going to sew me up, 'just like your mammy sews the clothes.'

She said, 'You have to be a very good girl and keep your mouth closed. There's nothing to be afraid of, sure haven't I just sewed your baby brother up.'

I felt a wave of delight. Maybe I would get to see Dermot after all! I still had the medal on the shoelace round my neck. I asked the doctor would she let me see my brother if I was a good girl. She told me to be very still until she was finished and then maybe I could see him. She worked on my face for what seemed like forever.

At last the doctor said, 'There you are, good as new, and in a few months' time you'll hardly notice the difference.'

She'd put forty-eight stitches on the inside of my mouth and, with another forty-eight, had sewed back the piece of skin that the garda had rescued from Rex's mouth. I couldn't talk properly and mumbled out the side of my mouth, asking if I could see Dermot now. The doctor told me not to talk and took off her red rubber apron.

'Not today darling,' she said, 'but we'll try and let you see him the next time you come. So keep your mouth closed and you'll be better soon.'

I got into an awful temper and as she came towards me I opened my mouth as wide as I could and screamed. The stitches burst and blood spurted out onto her white coat and then it was her turn to get into a temper.

'You're a very bold girl,' she told me. 'I have to do this all over again.'

I was definite about it: my mouth would not get sewed up if I could not see Dermot, and I told her so. One of the nurses gave in and promised to take me to him. But first I had to keep my mouth shut. I made the nurse swear on my sacred medal. The doctor sewed my mouth up again and this time the stitching stuck out the side of my face and I looked like a cat with whiskers.

All the while Mammy sat in a chair, crying softly. She kept saying over and over as she rocked back and forth, 'Oh God, what will Dessie say! Oh God, what will Dessie say!'

The nurse wrapped me in a big blanket, placed me in a chair with wheels, and took me to see Dermot. I almost wished she hadn't. One side of his little face looked raw and sore, and his right arm was completely covered by a large bandage. There were more bandages on both his legs. I cried, but I kept my mouth closed as I'd promised I would. I took the medal from around my neck and hung it from a bar over the cot. Then I held his tiny hand and begged God to make him better.

One of the neighbours came to the hospital on a big motorcycle with a sidecar. He put me in the sidecar and Mammy on the back, and off we went. When we got home, I was allowed to lie in Mammy and Daddy's bed, and Mammy got all the neighbours into the flat. I felt very important. Everyone stood around the bed, looking at me. I still held the two pennies that Mammy had given me for the eggs.

Then Daddy come in through the hall door. 'What the hell is going on now?' he said.

Mrs Sullivan told him to keep calm. 'It's not as bad as it looks, Dessie.'

She blessed herself as Daddy pushed past her to the bed. The women parted to let him through. No one spoke. Daddy looked at me and I tried to smile but it was too sore. Out of the corner of my mouth, I told him that I had seen Dermot. His face was very white and all the colour had gone from his lips. In a quiet voice, he asked Mammy what had happened.

'The Flynns' dog bit her,' she said, looking him full in the face. At least this time she knew she was telling the truth.

Daddy dashed out of the flat and a few seconds later I heard the other men telling him to go back inside and have a cup of tea.

'The Gardai are dealing with it,' they said. They wouldn't let him past the stairs and had to stop him jumping over the balcony to get down to the Flynns'.

'I'll kill the bastard thing with me own bare hands,' he was saying. 'Let me go!'

Two Gardai came in then and sat on either side of the bed. Out of the side of my mouth I told them, 'It wasn't Rex's fault. Mary was beating him with a chain and I wanted to make him better.'

One garda asked if I was sure it was Rex, and I nodded. They went down to the Flynns' then and discovered Rex in a trunk under a bed. Later, I found out they'd shot him.

After three days, I was able to open my fingers and let go of the pennies. But now I was afraid of dogs. Daddy took me to see *Lassie* at the pictures and, not long after that, he borrowed a dog that looked like Lassie and had me sit with it. I tried to be brave for as long as I could but I fainted. When I woke, the dog was gone.

Dermot stayed in hospital but he was getting better. Soon he would be home and we would be a family again. My mouth was starting to heal, I didn't need to take liquid food through a straw anymore. It was almost Christmas and that was exciting too, because Santy would visit with lovely presents for all of us.

First, though, Santy came to my school at Basin Street. There was to be a big party with jelly and ice cream and a present for everyone. We each had to give the nun a shilling when we went in. Mammy said she would meet me at the gate with the shilling. I waited and waited until it started to get dark and people were leaving the party. I knew she wasn't coming then and I wandered off home.

A few days before Christmas, Daddy told me to look after the boys. He was nipping out with Mammy for a while because it was Christmas. It was dark and we were all in bed when there was a knock at the front door. I went into the hall and saw, through the frosted window of the door, the figure of a man with a trilby hat. I thought it was Daddy and I opened the door, but two drunken men I'd never seen stumbled in past me. I screamed and hid under the blankets with Kevin and John. Noel and Maurice started screaming too and ran out of the flat and down to Mrs Sullivan's, in just their vests and their bare bums. I heard a commotion in the living room and then it was quiet. Mickey Sullivan came into the bedroom and told me they'd gone, but he said he'd stay until Daddy came home.

The following day the two men came to the door and apologised and gave us all a sixpence each. They'd got the right flat in the wrong block.

I don't remember much of Christmas Day, other than that it was a happy one. Mammy joined in a singsong with Granddad and Daddy. Granddad gave us each an orange, a sixpence, and a big slice of his home-made Christmas pudding. Dermot was coming home soon and we felt hopeful and happy. Daddy had lost his job a few days earlier, but he was sure he would get work for the Corporation in the new year. We could put this year behind us.

But 1953 wasn't finished with us!

TWO

St Stephen's Day dawned ordinarily enough. I was first out of bed, desperate to show my friend Angela the new dolly that Santy had brought me and to see if she'd got the roller skates she'd asked for. Everyone was still asleep and I crept as quietly as I could into the kitchen and cut a slice of Mammy's Christmas pudding. Then I slipped out of the front door and headed along the landing to Sullivans', but they were all still sleeping too. The rain was lashing down and the wind was howling. The landing was dry, though, and I decided to sit on our doorstep and wait for the others to wake up. I didn't have my coat on but I wasn't cold.

After a while Mammy came to the front door and asked what I was doing up at this ungodly hour.

'I'm waiting for Angela,' I said.

'Come in out of that,' she said, 'it's too early to be up. And you're not to wake Daddy.'

She was dressed up. It was still dark and I thought it must be a very early Mass she was going to. I promised I wouldn't make a sound, and she went back inside but left the door open a bit. I sat on the doorstep and every now and then I looked back and saw her legs in the hallway as she walked from room to room. She was tiptoeing so as not to wake the boys and Daddy.

It seemed like I sat there for a long time waiting for someone to stir at the Sullivans' flat. Finally, Mrs Sullivan came out. She asked me about Christmas and then headed off down the stairs. A couple of others from the upper landings passed, mostly women on their way to Mass.

Mammy came out again and stepped over me; she was carrying her big message bag. I was excited to see she was wearing her new red lipstick and the lovely shoes that Santy had brought her. She bent down and touched my shoulder. She had a queer look on her face.

'I want you to mind the babbies and mind yourself,' she said.

'Are you going to Mass?'

'No,' she said, 'I'm just going for the messages.' Then: 'Bye, bye.'

And she was gone. The heels of her shoes echoed in the stair hall. I stood up and looked over the balcony wall and saw her walking towards the grotto. I noticed that the message bag was full; something wasn't right.

'Mammy, wait for me!' I shouted. But she couldn't hear me through the rain and the wind.

I didn't bother going in to get my coat but dashed straight down the stairs and out into the storm. I knew I had to catch her somehow and I ran as fast as I could after her, shouting, 'Mammy, come back!'

I followed her to Dolphin's Barn Street. I could see her on the other side of the road but I couldn't cross, it was too busy. I was still screaming, 'Mammy! Mammy! Come back!' But she didn't turn around. I watched her get on a bus with a man.

I stood there for a few minutes, crying, not even noticing that I was soaked through to my skin. I have to tell Daddy, I thought, and I turned and ran back towards home. On the road leading into the flats, I crashed into someone and fell to the ground. When I looked up, I saw Mrs Sullivan towering over me.

'What the feck are ye tear arsing about at this time of the morning for?' she said.

She was wearing her usual short skirt and an enormous pair of pink bloomers. For a minute, her bloomers distracted me and I wanted to laugh. Then she bent down and her face softened.

'Ah, it's you, darling,' she said.

She picked me up off the ground and huddled me under her big dark coat. She smelled of Lifebuoy soap. I tried to wriggle loose. I said that Mammy was gone and I had to go tell Daddy.

'I know, pet,' she said. 'I know. God help yous.'

I got free and ran as fast as I could back to the flat. Daddy was still in bed, smoking a cigarette. There was a pain in my chest and I was breathless from running so fast. I stood beside the bed, dripping and sobbing.

Daddy was looking at me, saying, 'What is it, pet? What is it?'

When I caught my breath, I blurted out, 'She's gone!'

Daddy threw off the covers and leaped up out of bed. He knelt in front of me and tried to calm me down.

'Talk slowly and take deep breaths,' he said. 'Tell Daddy who's gone.'

'Mammy's gone, I followed her but she got on a bus with a man. I thought she was going for the messages. C'mon, Daddy, hurry up, we have to find her!'

I was tugging on his arms. I thought that if we hurried we might catch her and I tried to pull him to his feet, but Daddy looked like he couldn't move. He just knelt there.

Then he was up like a shot and rushing around the room. He pulled on his trousers, hooked the braces over his vest, put on his coat, and stuffed his bare feet into his shoes.

Just as we were coming out of the bedroom, Mrs Sullivan was walking into the flat.

She said, 'Dessie, I know what's happened, I saw her get on the bus. Take Evelyn with you and don't worry about the boys. Go see if you can find her mammy.'

Daddy grabbed my hand and dragged me behind him, back down the stairs and out to the car. It wouldn't start. Daddy was swearing and cursing. He got the starting handle from the boot and began winding up the engine until it came to life. He said nothing as he drove. The streets were deserted and it was still lashing and the little windscreen wiper could hardly keep up with the rain. We followed the bus route along Cork Street, down the Coombe, over to Dame Street and past Trinity College to the river. We crossed the Liffey and drove all the way up O'Connell Street, but there was no sign of the bus or Mammy.

Daddy turned out of town and headed towards the sea road. This meant we were going to Granny's and suddenly I felt glad because I loved Granny's. Daddy had first met Mammy at Granny's house when he was nineteen and got work there as a decorator. The house was big and right beside the sea and maybe Mammy would be there. All the rooms were full of lovely shiny furniture that we weren't allowed to touch. The back door opened onto a huge garden with an orchard in it, and Granny's kitchen always smelled of apples. Granny was very tall and she spoke quietly. She tied her hair in a bun at the back of her head and wore clean flowery aprons that had a scent of lavender. On her dresser she kept photographs of her grandchildren. All of them but us; Granny had no pictures of our family. Daddy had fallen out with her a long time ago. When he'd first married Mammy, they'd lived together in Granny's house for a little while, but one day Granny called him a cur and he never forgave her.

Sometimes Mammy took me on the bus to Dún Laoghaire and she'd sit in Granny's kitchen, crying.

'Marriage is a holy sacrament,' Granny would tell her, 'and with God's help you'll get through it.'

I didn't know what Granny was on about, but Mammy cried easily, so I was used to it and took no notice. Mostly, visits to Granny were happy times. We would play in the orchard or go out to the pier to watch the boats going to England.

Now, I was on my way to Granny's again but, as we drove along, the look on Daddy's face made me think that this visit wouldn't be a happy one. We pulled up outside the house and ran as fast as we could up the long path to the black front door. The door was glossy from the rain. Daddy banged on it with his fist and rang the bell at the same time. He was cursing when Granny opened the door. She had her hat and coat on and her shiny brown shoes, as if she was just heading out.

'Desmond! What on earth is going on? I thought it was the devil himself at the door. Come in out of the weather.'

When Daddy pushed past her, he almost knocked her against the wall, and I felt ashamed of him treating Granny that way.

'Where's the fecking bitch?' he said.

He was snarling like an angry dog, like Rex after he'd

bitten my face. I'd never seen Daddy like this. It wasn't like when Dermot got burned. I was afraid and I ran to Granny and hid behind her skirt.

'Mind your tone and your language,' Granny said. She told him to calm down or leave. Granny wasn't afraid of anyone. 'You're in my home now, not some back street public house.'

She took off her coat and hat and hung them carefully in the hall press and put on one of her flowery pinafores. She lit the stove and set a kettle of water on to boil. Daddy was smoking a cigarette by then, puffing away like a dragon while Granny brought her delicate china cups and saucers to the table.

'Never mind the tea,' Daddy said, 'I want to know where that bitch of a daughter of yours is. She's run off with her fancy man…'

Granny covered her face with her crinkly hands. 'I don't believe it,' she said.

'…and if I get hold of her, I'll kill her, so I will.'

Granny sat down heavily at the table. 'She wouldn't leave the children, especially the baby. Sure, he's still in hospital.'

But she sounded like she was talking to herself. Granny'd had seventeen children and Mammy had been the last. With Granny's help, all the children had done well for themselves; even Mammy had been given a trade. She'd served her apprenticeship as a master confectioner, but when she'd married Daddy, against Granny's wishes, she'd had to give it up.

Daddy banged his fist on the table, making Granny jump. 'I want to know where she is, do you hear?'

Granny didn't know where Mammy was. She wanted Daddy to leave the house. She said she would telephone the rest of the family and would let Daddy know if she found out anything.

'If she doesn't turn up by tonight,' she said, 'I'll come over to the flat and look after the children. And if she can't be found, we'll have to make arrangements. Evelyn and Noel can come to me, and I'm sure my other daughters can help with the youngest.'

Daddy yanked me out of the chair and half dragged me down the long hallway. He threw open the door. As we left the house, he shouted over his shoulder, 'You and yours will never see my children again!'

I'd been frightened but now I started to cry. Daddy looked down at me and his expression softened. He put his arm around me and hugged me close to him, there on the footpath outside of Granny's.

'I'm sorry, pet,' he said, 'I didn't mean to frighten you.'

All through that long wet miserable day, Daddy drove round to all the members of his family and to his friends and then to anyone else he could think of. When it was getting dark, we stopped somewhere in the country. I didn't know where we were but I thought Daddy must be visiting a friend. He left me in the car and told me I was to stay there till he came back.

I was sitting in the car waiting for him when I felt eyes all around me. I had only ever seen one cow before and that was a poor old beast that stood in the shed near the flats. For three pence, a man would fill your jug with creamy milk straight from the udder. Now, there was a whole herd of cows and they'd surrounded the car and were peering in at me. I screamed and screamed but their big liquid brown eyes wouldn't go away.

Daddy came back and chased them off and I told him how brave he was, but he just laughed and called me a silly old thing. He headed the little black car back towards the city. The rain was still coming down and the streets were empty. Daddy stopped outside his uncle's house. Even though he was Daddy's uncle, I called him Grandfather Brady. When I was in hospital with scarlet fever, Grandfather Brady had made me a beautiful dolls' house with carpets and electric lights. I loved him nearly as much as I loved my own granddad.

The house was almost completely dark. Grandfather Brady and his wife, Aunt Agnes, were sitting by the fire, smoking cigarettes. There was one light on in the small room, a bare bulb hanging from the ceiling. When Daddy told them he was looking for Mammy, they looked at each other nervously and seemed to tense up. Aunt Agnes put her head in her hands just like Granny had and started crying loudly.

'God forgive me, Dessie,' she said, 'but you should have seen it coming. Or have you been walking around blind?'

Grandfather Brady told her to be quiet. 'Put the kettle on,' he said.

We found out that Mammy had gone off with Grandfather Brady's son – Daddy's cousin, Gerry. Grandfather Brady knew they were going to run away, and he'd tried to persuade Gerry not to do it. He asked him what kind of a woman would carry on with her husband's cousin, she with six kids and all. Grandfather Brady couldn't tell Daddy very much; all he really knew was that the two of them had gone to Scotland.

'I'm sorry, son,' he said. 'If I could do anything to get her back, I would.'

Daddy got up. He didn't want the cup of tea, he just wanted to leave.

As Grandfather Brady showed us out of the hall door, he patted Daddy's back and said, 'It'll be a long time before I have Gerry in this house again.'

The flat was cold and empty when we came home. The boys were still with the neighbours. Daddy lit a fire on the small grate in the living room and tore off what was left of the lino to keep it going. The flames cast eerie shadows on the bare walls. We sat in silence watching the fire, each of us in our own misery. Daddy hadn't eaten all day and I found a piece of the Christmas pudding and gave it to him, but he didn't touch it. It was hard to believe it was only yesterday that Mammy had served the pudding after dinner and we'd all clapped and cheered as she set it on fire and carried it into the living room.

Daddy went to his room and brought back three biscuit tins and set them beside the fire. When he lifted the lid off one of the tins, I saw that it was full of photographs of our family.

Daddy took lots of photographs. He used the bathroom as a darkroom to develop them himself. He had a red bulb in there and he hung the pictures over the bath. I'd often seen the boys standing outside the door with their legs crossed, hopping about, shouting that they needed the toilet. And Daddy would shout back, 'Don't open the door!'

Now, I watched him as he emptied the biscuit tins, the little black and white pictures forming three mounds on the floor. I couldn't believe what I saw. He had a big pair of scissors and he picked up each photograph in turn and, with a quick snip, cut Mammy out of every single one of them and threw the bits of her onto the fire. The flames turned a pretty blue and yellow every time Daddy added another piece of a picture. I saw one large photograph lying apart from the pile and I picked it up. It was of Mammy and Daddy. Their arms were linked and they were smiling happily out at me. Mammy looked lovely. She was wearing a big hat and there were flowers in the lapel of her jacket. In Daddy's lapel, there was a white carnation.

'Can I keep this one?' I said. 'Mammy's so pretty in it and I want to remember what she looks like.'

'No,' he said, 'you can't!'

He snatched the picture from me. He stared at it for a long time. Then his whole body began to convulse and tears ran down his cheeks. It was the first time I had ever seen him cry. Without a word, he began to cut Mammy out of this picture too and then he threw her tiny figure on the fire. I shrank back into the chair, clutching my knees to my chest.

'Is Mammy dead?' I whispered.

Daddy didn't answer right away. I think he'd forgotten I was there. Then he looked up at me where I was crouched in the chair and leaned over and lifted me onto his knee. Holding me close, he said quietly into my ear, 'No, pet, she's not dead, but she might as well be.'

He paused because he was sobbing again.

Then he said, 'Forget her. We won't see her anymore.'

He didn't weep for Mammy after that and I never heard him speak of her again, except to say he would kill her if he ever saw her again.

The next morning we went to the Garda station on Pearse Street. Daddy hadn't been in a Garda station since the day he had been in an ID parade. They'd paid him five shillings to stand in the line wearing fake spectacles. The man who'd been robbed paced up and down the line and finally stopped at Daddy.

'That's yer man,' he declared, pointing. 'I'm sure of it!'

Daddy got a fright, but the garda thought it was funny.

We hesitated for a moment outside the building. It was so big it made even Daddy look small. Inside, we found a thin, bald garda writing at his desk. Daddy told him that Mammy was missing and that he didn't know where she was.

'I've got six children,' he said. 'You have to help me find her.'

The garda looked up from his journal 'It's not a police matter. Go and see the cruelty man.' He pointed with his pencil at the door. 'Molesworth Street.'

As we were walking towards the door, Daddy called over his shoulder, 'Thanks very much for feck all, you long skinny drink of water.'

Back outside, we walked around the front of Trinity College, past the tall gates and the Provost's house, the big buildings that Daddy said were the only good things to come out of 'the bastard English'. On Molesworth Street, we found a green door that opened up onto a narrow flight of wooden stairs. When we reached the landing,

Daddy stood staring at the door. There was a sign on it that said KNOCK and WAIT and, above that, the initials NSPCC were etched in black on a shiny brass plate. This was where the 'cruelty man' worked.

Daddy took a deep breath and followed the instructions. The inspector who came to the door was a large plump man with a ruddy face. He recognized us immediately, and we remembered him too. He was Mr Wogan, who'd been at our house after Dermot was burned. He sat down behind a large green leather-covered desk and invited us to sit. He looked surprised. He didn't often get men in his office. Usually, he said, his clients were women who couldn't care for their broods after their husbands had gone across the water to earn a decent pay packet. A few sent English pound notes without even a letter. Mostly the men never came back and often the children ended up in the industrial schools.

While Mr Wogan was talking, I looked out of the big window at the Mansion House and thought how lovely and grand it was compared to Fatima Mansions. Daddy sat perched on the edge of a wooden chair, turning his trilby hat in his hands. When Mr Wogan finished speaking, Daddy explained that his wife had gone off with his cousin to Scotland and he had no reason to believe she was coming back.

'I don't want the feckin bitch back now,' he said, 'but I have six kids to look after.'

I was shocked to hear Daddy say that about Mammy but I was still half thinking about how strange it was that even though the flats and the Mansion House were so different, they were both called mansions.

'I've no job and no money, so I'm asking for your advice. What do I do now?'

Daddy was hoping to start work with the Corporation at the end of January but now that Mammy was gone he would have to look after us and wouldn't be able to go to work. Mr Wogan smiled kindly and offered Daddy a Sweet Afton. He said he was sure that Mammy would come home after she'd kicked up her heels a bit. Surely no mother would leave her children for long? Not in his experience, anyway.

'Have you got anyone who can help you?' Mr Wogan asked. 'Mother? Sisters?'

Daddy shook his head. 'No one.'

He told Mr Wogan that his mammy had died when he was thirteen and his sister Margaret not long after that, of meningitis, and his only other sister Annie had died too, four years ago, from tuberculosis.

'Going round trying to sell scenty soap to dirty oul ones in the tenements,' he said.

Annie's husband Milo had gone to jail. Milo had been the treasurer of the painters' union and was arrested for stealing the union funds. Daddy never forgave him for leaving Annie alone to look after their little boy.

Mr Wogan pressed his fingertips together and tapped his chin.

'Surely you have someone,' he said. 'What about your wife's family?'

'Never!' Daddy roared, jumping from his chair.

Mr Wogan stood up and held out his hands to calm Daddy.

'All right,' he said. 'Just a thought.' He motioned for Daddy to sit down again and offered him another Sweet Afton.

'Have you thought about any long-term arrangements for the children?' he asked.

Daddy didn't answer. Mr Wogan lit his own cigarette and stared out of the window, thinking. Finally, he said, 'If your wife doesn't come back, I think we'll have to have the children committed to the industrial schools.'

Daddy had been pacing back and forth in front of Mr Wogan's desk. Now he stopped and turned sharply on his heel.

'I wouldn't have her back if Jesus himself asked me!' he spat. He stubbed out his cigarette in the heavy ashtray and started pacing again, muttering, 'My poor kids, my poor kids.'

He had no money to pay a child minder and the only female relative he had apart from Mammy's family was Aunt Agnes. But Aunt Agnes was Gerry's mother and Gerry was off with Mammy and there was no way Daddy was going to ask Aunt Agnes.

'So,' he said wearily, 'it will have to be the schools. But just until I can get myself together.'

Mr Wogan looked at my daddy with pity, but then he tried to put on a bright face.

'Well,' he said, 'first things first. We'll get the sisters up off their knees. I'll arrange for them to call to you tomorrow morning, and they'll look after the children until we can make more permanent arrangements.'

He took out some official documents and Daddy signed them.

When we left the office, Daddy put me on a bus and told me to go to Mrs Sullivan, who would give me a bit of dinner. He promised he wouldn't be long.

'Are you sending me to the magdalen's, Daddy?'

He patted my head and held my face up to his.

'Don't you worry yourself,' he said. 'Go look after the boys.'

The bus drove off, leaving Daddy standing alone on the pavement.

Daddy wandered aimlessly that afternoon, through a cold north wind he told me years later. He wasn't a religious man at all, but he was speaking to God, pleading for help. He had a half crown in his pocket, all that was left from Christmas. His National Assistance money wasn't due for another three days. Standing in front of Mulligan's on Poolbeg Street, he heard sounds of laughter and merriment coming from inside. He pushed the door open with his shoulder and, for as long as the half crown lasted, put aside his worries. He played the piano and sang.

Just after seven the next morning, the Sisters of Mercy swooped on our flat.

'Like a feckin flock of blackbirds,' Daddy muttered. To the nuns, he said, 'Thanks Sisters, I'll leave it to you. I've to go and look for a job and I'll be back after dinnertime.'

Daddy was only saying that. He couldn't go looking for a job, it wasn't even the new year yet. He was going to the pub to get out of the way of the nuns. Noel and Maurice tried to sneak out of the room after him, but one of the nuns dragged them back.

'You're going nowhere but the bath tub, me boyos,' she laughed.

I was hiding under the blanket with John and Kevin, but the nuns found us. They scrubbed all five of us with Lifebuoy till we shone pink and then started on the flat. They looked grim and determined and, as they cleaned, they said many prayers and called on the Virgin Mary and whatever saints they could think of. Afterwards, we all sat down to a clean table and ate hot stew and freshly baked bread. For the next couple of weeks, two of the sisters visited us each day with food and clothes and clean bedding. I prayed every night that God would send Mammy back, but I never told Daddy about my prayers.

It was a Sunday night and, except for Dermot, who was still in hospital, we were all in the big bed. Daddy was kneeling on the floor beside us. We were singing our songs and he was telling us stories his mammy had told him when he was a boy. He knew that this was the last night we would all be together. When we started getting sleepy, Daddy kissed each of our heads in turn and crept out of the room. I didn't sleep right away and I could hear him from where I lay in the bed. He was sitting in the darkened living room, crying.

The next morning, the nuns arrived early with new clothes for all of us. I got new shoes, too, and all the boys got boots. They marched around the table in single file, swinging their arms up and down like soldiers, their boots making the furniture tremble.

> *Shoulder to shoulder*
> *together standing strong*
> *to answer Ireland's call*

Daddy let them go on with their noisy singing and stomping until Mrs Flynn down below banged on the ceiling and shouted, 'Jaysus, Dessie, can ye give us a little peace down here!'

Daddy put his finger to his lips and gave a gentle 'sshhh' to the boys. He was smiling, so I knew he wasn't cross, but I didn't join in the game anyway. Something was going to happen today and I was dreading it.

When it was time to go, we followed Daddy down the steps. He was carrying John and Kevin. The neighbours were standing in the street. Some were crying, some praying, and most were blessing themselves. The men patted Daddy on the back.

'Take heart Dessie,' they told him. 'You'll get them home soon enough.'

'God bless the poor little innocents!' a woman shouted.

Daddy piled us all into the Austin. I didn't see Fatima Mansions until many years later.

I sat on one of the long wooden benches that lined three walls of the bare waiting room of the Children's Court, hugging John and Kevin. Daddy had told us that he wouldn't be long and we sat still and silent, waiting for him. A big funny man in a uniform tried to make us laugh. He was the usher. He pulled a two shilling piece from behind his ear and Noel and Maurice were very impressed by this small miracle. Noel climbed onto the bench beside the man and pulled his ears forward, searching for more coins. The usher laughed.

'They're not there, little man, but maybe they're here!'

By magic, he pulled a sixpence from behind Noel's ear. My brothers had a new hero. The usher came over to where I was sitting. He bent down on his hunkers and tried to make me laugh, but I wouldn't even smile.

'Where's my Daddy?' I asked him.

Even though I didn't understand what was happening, I knew deep down we weren't going home. The nice man looked at me with a sad face.

'C'mon, little old woman,' he said, 'give us a smile, even a small one will do.' He tickled me under the chin. I liked him, but I couldn't smile.

'I'll tell you what I'll do,' he said. 'I'll go and find out what's going on and see if there's a bottle of lemonade somewhere. Will that do you?'

I nodded my thanks. I couldn't speak then because I was going to cry and I didn't want to. I wanted to be brave for my brothers. The usher got to his feet with great difficulty and went to the door.

'Now be good children,' he said, 'and I'll see if I can find sweets for us all.'

He went out of the door and when he closed it behind him, I heard the key turning in the lock. I put John and Kevin on the floor and ran to the door and tried to open it. I started kicking the door and screaming for Daddy. All the boys gathered around me and were tugging at my dress and crying.

Then I heard Daddy. He was yelling at someone out in the corridor. 'Open the fecking door, you bastards!'

He started kicking the door. I was trying to pull it open from inside and everyone was screaming and crying louder and calling for Daddy. I thought that if we didn't get the door open quick, the men would make Daddy go away and I'd never see him again.

Then everything went quiet in the corridor and I shushed my brothers. I could hear Mr Wogan from the NSPCC saying, 'Desmond, this won't help the children. Try and make it easy for them.'

The door swung open and the room was suddenly filled with people. A nun with a big winged wimple stood next to Mr Wogan and another usher in a uniform was there, along with the funny man who'd done the tricks with the shillings.

And Dermot was there! Daddy was holding him. He still had bandages on his arms, but he'd got bigger since I'd last seen him. Daddy handed Dermot to me and he lifted Kevin and hugged him tight. There were tears running down Daddy's face. The nun took Kevin from Daddy and Daddy took Dermot back from me and handed him to Mr Wogan. It was all very confusing but then I realised at once what was going on. These people were taking my two baby brothers away. I grabbed Mr Wogan's trouser leg and screamed.

'You can't take the babies!'

Daddy picked me up and held me tight. The other three boys clung to his legs. We were all crying, the nun too, and even the men were in tears. The funny man blew his nose very noisily and said to no one in particular, 'Will that woman ever know the pain she has caused here today?'

One of the men managed to tear the boys away from Daddy's side. Daddy put me down and took my hand and we followed the court officer and my brothers outside. An enormous black car was waiting at the bottom of the courthouse steps. Mr Wogan led my brothers to the car. Daddy let go of my hand and ran over to them. He knelt down on the path and hugged all my brothers together. He was crying again and the boys were too. Mr Wogan put his hand on Daddy's shoulder.

'C'mon, Des,' he said, 'make it easy for them.'

Daddy stood up and took a deep breath.

'Look, boys!' he said, trying to make it all into a big adventure. 'It's just like Al Capone's car, how lucky can you get? In you go, and you're not to be shooting the nuns in Kilkenny.' Then he kissed them one by one and put them in the car.

Daddy and I stood on the path, watching the black car move silently away. The boys were waving at us. I could see their tiny frightened faces through the back window. Even after the car disappeared, we stayed standing there. I thought maybe there'd been a mistake and that the car would come back any minute. But finally, Daddy led me away.

When we got to our own car, he told me that he was taking me to the convent at High Park. He didn't say anything during the short journey and I made myself as small as I could in the seat beside him. Soon, we pulled up in front of some huge black iron gates that led up a long gravel drive. I leaned forward in the seat to see more. On either side of the drive were beautiful neat lawns and little islands of flowerbeds. At the top of the drive was the convent, which was attached to the chapel. On the other side of the chapel was another red brick building with bars on the windows, like the prison near Granddad's house on

Innisfallen Parade. I didn't know it yet, but that was the women's penitentiary; the building beyond it was the 'Lunatic Asylum'.

The car made a loud crunching sound on the red gravel as Daddy pulled up outside the double doors of the convent. I started to shake and crouched as low as I could in the seat and made myself into a ball.

'Come on, pet,' Daddy said, 'don't let them see you're frightened.'

He got out of the car and opened my door, but I refused to go and pleaded with him not to make me.

He reached into the car and lifted me out and set me on my feet. Then he straightened his tie, cleared his throat and, taking me firmly by the hand, led me to the door. He pulled a chain on the wall and I could hear a bell sounding somewhere far away.

A nun dressed all in white opened the big door and smiled at us. She knew who we were.

'You must be Mr Doyle and Evelyn,' she said. 'Please follow me.'

Inside, she bowed her head and led us down a long hallway. On both sides of the wide passage, there were life-sized statues of saints on pedestals. The sound of our shoes on the tiles echoed around our heads. Eventually, we came to a large room at the end of the passage and the nun told us to be seated.

'Reverend Mother will be with you shortly,' she said, and left us alone.

All along one wall of the room, there were windows that went from the ceiling to the floor. The floor was so shiny you could see a reflection of yourself, as if you were standing on water. A weak January sun came through the windows in wide straight shafts. It was all marvellous and made me think of a picture I had seen of a very grand ball where the ladies wore gowns with big skirts and the men wore red and gold army uniforms. The *Blue Danube* was running through my head. I knew it because Daddy played it often on the piano in his special room and sometimes I sat in and listened.

'Pay attention, Evelyn!'

A strict-looking nun had appeared and clapped her hands twice as she scolded me. I ran over and clung to the back of Daddy's leg.

'It would be better for her if you go quickly, Mr Doyle,' the nun said.

Daddy knelt down on one knee and held me at arms' length.

'Now, pet, I have to go. But I'll be back very soon and we'll get the boys and we'll all be together again. Be a good girl,' he whispered. He told me that he loved me and that he wouldn't leave me here any longer than he had to. 'That's a promise.'

Then he stood up and said to the nun, 'You're not to cut her hair, do you hear me?'

I tried to follow him out the door, crying for him not to go, but the nun caught me and held me. Daddy didn't look back as he left the room, but I saw his shoulders shaking and I knew he was crying again.

I was alone now. The nun took my wrist and pulled me behind her, telling me 'the rules' as she yanked me along.

'And you address all the sisters as Mother,' she said.

She handed me over to two nuns who wore snow-white

aprons that completely covered their habits.

Mother Imelda and Mother Bernadette led me up the wide wooden staircase to the dormitory. I hadn't seen a room as big as this one since the day I'd been to the baths at Bride Street. Along two of the walls that faced each other were rows of narrow iron beds. Between them in the centre of the room was a long table. There was a large enamel basin on the table and, opposite each bed, a glass, a toothbrush, and a folded towel. The floor was red lino and it shone. The room gave me the shivers. It reminded me of the hospital ward I had been in when I'd had scarlet fever.

'This will be your bed,' Mother Imelda said, pointing to the one nearest the door.

She handed me a long coat that was made of the same material towels are and told me to go into the bathroom and take off my clothes. It seemed that every time I saw a nun or a nurse now I had to take off my clothes. This time, I refused. When the two nuns couldn't persuade me to do as I was told, one of them went into the bathroom. I could hear water running. Oh no, I thought. I wondered if my brothers would be having a bath too and for a moment I felt happy thinking about what they might be putting the nuns in Kilkenny through. They dragged me into the bathroom and got me out of my clothes. The water was blistering hot and I howled, but they scrubbed away at me.

'Cleanliness is next to Godliness,' Mother Imelda said, and I thought that if that was true then my brothers and I must have been very far from God.

When the bath was over, Mother Imelda handed me a bundle of clothes and told me she would wait just outside the door.

'In case you get stuck,' she said.

I spread the clothes on a bench in the bathroom. The vest and knickers I recognized, but what in the name of God was this? It was like a very short jacket with no sleeves in it and it was made from a rough woolly cream-coloured material. It had big rubber buttons down the front. I decided to keep it till last. I put on the black frock with the yellow bodice and the long thick brown stockings and the boots with the metal studs on the soles. And then, over everything, I put on the woolly thing and buttoned it up to the neck. When I presented myself to the two nuns, they both put their hands to their mouths.

'Oh, child!' Mother Imelda cried.

They were trying not to laugh, I could tell, and I got annoyed with them and demanded to know what was so funny. Mother Bernadette knelt before me and started to unfasten the jacket. She was laughing out loud by then.

'Evelyn, it's a chemise and it goes over your vest, dear, not your dress. It helps to keep your chest warm,' she explained.

They fixed my chemise and led me back down the stairs and along another corridor until we stopped outside a door. I could hear girls laughing and talking and dishes rattling on the other side. Mother Bernadette threw open the door and clapped her hands twice. Instantly, there was quiet. We were in the refectory. It was filled with long bare wooden tables that had benches either side of them. It looked like there were hundreds of girls in the room. Every one of them was dressed exactly like me. They all had pudding basin haircuts, except one or two who had no hair at all. On the tables, there were big white enamel jugs full of steaming hot cocoa and plates of bread and butter. All the girls turned round together to look at me, and I felt sick and frightened.

Mother Imelda called out, 'Siobhán O'Neill!'

A girl of about fourteen got up from one of the tables and walked quickly towards us.

'You will take care of Evelyn,' Mother Imelda said. 'She's our new girl, and you're to tell her what to do and make sure she understands the rules properly.'

She gave me a little push in the direction of Siobhán.

Siobhán smiled at me; I liked her straight away. Her skin was very white and she had deep blue eyes and jet-black shiny hair. She led me to her table and told the others to bunch up and make a space for me. Everyone obeyed her. She poured cocoa into one of the enamel cups and passed it to me.

'I don't like cocoa,' I said. 'I want tea.'

Some of the girls at the table sniggered, but Siobhán shushed them.

'We only get tea at breakfast,' she said, 'but I'll try to get you some milk.'

I started to cry. I didn't like this place where you couldn't even get a cup of tea. Siobhán assured me that I would get used to it. She said there was even some gas to be had when the nuns weren't looking.

The rest of the evening passed in a blur. Everyone was rushing around, as though they all had something important to do. I stuck close to Siobhán until it was time to go into the big room, the one where I'd last seen Daddy. We all knelt down in rows on the bare floor while a sour-faced nun led us through the rosary. My knees hurt and it seemed like the rosary went on forever.

When it was finally bedtime, Siobhán showed me which bowl was mine on the big table and how we all had to take turns filling the basins with warm water from the jugs that stood in a row in the bathroom. On my bed there was a long white flannel nightdress. I had never seen a night-dress before and when I asked what it was for, some of the girls laughed. Once we were all in our nightdresses, Mother Bernadette came in to inspect the dormitory while we knelt beside our bed to say prayers.

'God bless our mammies and daddies and our brothers and sisters.'

The words reminded me of why I was there and I started to cry, but just a little. Mother Bernadette tucked me into bed and assured me everything would be all right. She told me that my brothers and my Daddy would be looked after by God.

I was clean and warm and not hungry, but I wanted to be back in the flat at Fatima Mansions. I wanted my baby brothers beside me. I was lying on my stomach, crying into the pillow and thinking about them, when my covers were whipped off. A strange nun glared down at me.

'We do not sleep in that disgusting position!' she roared.

She turned me on my back very roughly, crossed my arms over my chest and said, '*This* is how we sleep, so as not to tempt the devil!'

With that, she threw the covers back over me and left me there, terrified.

How could the devil get past all these nuns, I wondered. How could he be tempted if I wasn't lying on my back? And sure, hadn't we all been praying since the minute we got here? Grace before and after tea, the rosary before bed-time, and more prayers right before getting into bed. The devil surely was not welcome here.

When I finally fell asleep, I dreamed of the devil and poor Rex the dog, and of Mammy going away as she ran farther and farther down the road.

Daddy didn't go straight back to the flat that first night after they'd taken us away from him. He couldn't bear to be alone, so he went to Granddad's house. Daddy was all Granddad had left in the world. When Daddy was young, Granddad had put him into music school. Daddy's oldest sister Margaret was a concert pianist and Granddad him-self had played the lead cello for more than thirty years with the orchestra at the Gaiety Theatre. But Daddy'd left the school when he was offered an apprenticeship as a painter and decorator with Michael Feeney's firm. Granddad had tried to persuade him to carry on with his music studies, but Daddy'd been impatient to earn money. And then he'd met Mammy.

Now, as he stood there looking at Daddy, Granddad didn't know how to ease Daddy's pain, and his heart ached.

Grandma Doyle had died when Daddy was just thirteen. Granddad had carved a headstone for her grave out of a large rock he'd taken from her beloved garden. The official at the cemetery had told him that the headstone didn't conform to regulations. Undeterred, Granddad had got Daddy out of bed in the middle of the night and together they'd loaded the rock onto a handcart and pushed it to the cemetery. Granddad had jumped the railing, and he and Daddy had managed to haul the headstone, which weighed fifty or sixty pounds, over the rails. They marked Grandma Doyle's grave with it and Granddad never visited the cemetery again. He trusted that his wife was at peace in heaven.

Daddy had run wild after his mother's death. Granddad, although he was eccentric, had wanted a peaceful life, and found it hard looking after an adolescent boy on his own. In the end, he and Daddy had managed, partly by learning to stay out of each other's way.

Now Granddad wanted a peaceful old age. He looked at his son and sighed. He quoted Shakespeare,

> *Sorrow breaks seasons and the reposing hours,*
> *Makes the night morning,*
> *and the noontide night.*

Granddad was always quoting from literature. Sometimes he translated lines from Shakespeare into the Irish, often with interesting results. He squeezed Daddy's shoulder and said, 'Here, Dessie. Go get a drink and relax a bit.'

He handed Daddy a ten shilling note, and Daddy set off on foot to find a quiet pub where he could forget his misery.

A few hours later, Daddy staggered up the stairs of the flats. It was well past midnight by then. He'd got into company in the pub and started on the rum. It was the only drink that could have him on the floor and, as a rule, he never touched it. But that night was an exception. Inside the flat, he collapsed on the big bed and, for the first time in weeks, slept soundly.

The next morning, he was cold and confused when he woke; for a few seconds, he wondered if he'd had a nightmare. He put the kettle on to boil and lit a cigarette. He made tea in a jam jar. He shaved and washed himself. Then he pulled Granddad's battered old suitcase from underneath the bed and threw what clothes he had into it, along with whatever photographs were left and all of our birth certificates. He packed his white overalls, too, and the canvas bag that held his paint brushes and tools, and he fastened the case with twine. The things from his special room, including the Hornby train set that Santy had brought the boys, he placed into boxes. Then he put the whole lot in the boot of the black Austin.

Before he left, he went next door to Mrs Sullivan's flat. She ushered him in, swatting good-naturedly at her brood with her old slipper as she led Daddy down the hallway.

'Get out of it, you fecking ruffians,' she screeched.

Then she turned to Daddy and said, 'Can I help?' There was concern in her voice.

Daddy asked her to take the keys to the flat and bring them back to the Corporation for him, and he told her that if there was anything she wanted from the flat, she could take it.

'You can get a few bob for the piano and the china cabinet,' he said. 'But most of it isn't even fit for the Liffey.'

Mrs Sullivan offered him a cup of tea, but he refused.

'Thanks for all your trouble,' Daddy said. 'Now I'm getting out of this shithole.'

They said their goodbyes. As Daddy started towards the stairs, Mrs Sullivan blessed herself and said, 'God be with you, son.'

'Well, He hasn't bothered Himself with me much lately, has He?' Daddy called over his shoulder.

Then he drove to Granddad's house.

'I'm going to England,' he announced. 'There's work and good wages there.'

He handed Granddad a scrap of paper. It was an advert he'd clipped out of the newspaper. PAINTERS WANTED – GOOD RATES. It gave an address in Yorkshire, England. As Daddy watched Granddad reading the advert, he broke down. Granddad stood helplessly by, waiting for Daddy's tears to subside. Even though it was still morning, he handed him a short measure of brandy and told him to steady himself. Daddy felt a bit better for having had the cry and the brandy, and he assured Granddad that he was all right.

'I'm ready to go,' he said. 'I'll write when I get a place over there. Will you visit Evelyn for me? Keep an eye on how she's doing?'

Granddad went with Daddy to the pier at Dún Laoghaire. They shook hands before Daddy got on the mail boat, and Granddad put a ten pound note in Daddy's top pocket. Neither of them spoke.

Daddy leaned on the rail of the boat as it steamed away from Dublin. He could see the solitary figure of Granddad, standing apart from the crowd of young wives and families that had gathered. Daddy felt sorry for the women on the pier. Some of them had several small children with them. The children wore threadbare coats; they had braved the cold to see their daddies going off across the water. Even as the boat moved away, Daddy imagined himself already back in Dublin, surrounded by his children.

He stayed on deck long after Dublin had disappeared. Below deck, the men were keeping each other company, but Daddy didn't feel sociable. He took out the scrap of paper with the advert on it. The address was for a place called Holmfirth, in Yorkshire. He'd no idea where Yorkshire was, let alone Holmfirth.

THREE

Daddy was in England all that spring and through the long summer. The boys were still in Kilkenny and I was at the convent. Daddy sent letters and parcels and the nuns let me take the parcels out onto the playing field, where the other girls would gather round, squealing, as excited as I was. Whenever Daddy sent lollipops, he always included enough for the others.

It hadn't taken me long to settle into the routine of the convent. I learned early on that it was best to do as you were told and blend into the crowd. Apart from Mother Paul, I liked most of the nuns. Mother Paul took the choir and sometimes led us in prayers. She often scolded me for my refusal to 'exalt the Lord', and my knees were red-raw from praying for forgiveness.

From the grounds of the convent we could see the penitentiary and the asylum. They were part of High Park, along with the convent. Most of us were in the convent because we were orphans or because our parents were destitute or had abandoned us, and most of us would stay there until we were sixteen and old enough to get work in the city. In the convent, we worked in the laundry and on the farm, which was on the convent grounds. Sometimes, women from the pen worked in the laundry with us and, occasionally, we'd catch a glimpse of one of the 'lunatics' standing in the window of the asylum. But we didn't pass any heed; we just thought of them as our neighbours.

All the girls over the age of six went to Lark Hill School outside the convent. The nuns lined us up in a long crocodile and shepherded us through the farm and the orchard until we came out of a small green gate onto Collins Avenue. Many of the girls at Lark Hill who lived at home wouldn't have much to do with those of us from the convent. Our uniforms were different and we wore green cloaks and black leather hob-nailed boots, and our families, if we had any, were gone away somewhere. I made friends with a couple of girls who weren't in the convent, but we couldn't let the teachers know; they disapproved of such friendships.

After school, we traipsed back to the convent and began our chores. Sometimes I worked on the farm. I helped to churn the butter and boil up the mash for the pigs and I rounded up the chickens and put them into the coop at the end of the afternoon. When I couldn't get them all in, I pulled my hair and screamed in frustration.

'Have patience, my child,' Mother Bridget would say, smiling.

And I would wonder where you got this thing called patience, and what it looked like.

I liked working on the farm, and my reward each day was a big glass of rich creamy milk. My life would've been happy if I weren't missing Daddy and my brothers so much. I saved the comics that Granddad brought me and sent them to the boys along with letters I'd written. But Mother Aloysius told me that it was not a good idea to be upsetting them.

'Better to wait until you are all together again,' she said.

Granny came to visit every Sunday from Dún Laoghaire

and brought me green ribbons for my hair and ¼lb packets of Barry's tea. On St Patrick's Day she brought a lovely bunch of shamrock. Her presents made me feel very grand. I especially loved the ribbons. I had always worn them and they reminded me of my life before the convent.

Sometimes when Granny came to the convent with the tea and ribbons, she would find Granddad – Daddy's father – there. They wouldn't sit together and it was very complicated trying to divide my time between them; I loved them both. In my stockinged feet, I would slide up and down the visiting room, from Granny to Granddad and back again.

Once or twice in the summer, Alfie Byrne, the Lord Mayor of Dublin, came with a big bus and the nuns filled the laundry baskets with sandwiches and we had a great day at the seaside. Alfie Byrne had a thick moustache that was twirled at the ends. I wondered if he pasted it on every morning. He joined in the fun at the beach and on the way back to the convent, would lead a singsong on the bus. It made me think of Daddy, who would have loved the singing.

One Friday after school had been let out, I was playing in the orchard with my friends when I heard Mother Bridget calling my name. I started up the path that connected the farm to the orchard and bumped right into her as she came running towards me.

'Quick, child!' She took my cloak and schoolbag and pushed me on my way. 'Go as fast as you can to the Reverend Mother's office. You have a very special visitor.'

'Daddy!' I cried.

I knew it was Daddy, it had to be. He'd told me he would

come. Siobhán was always saying that her daddy was going to come. But Siobhán had been at the convent since she was two, and he hadn't come yet. When I said my prayers at night and asked God to make my daddy come back, I asked Him to send Siobhán's daddy as well.

I reached the Reverend Mother's office and skidded to a halt on the shiny floor. I had been running so fast I nearly ran right past her door. I stopped to catch my breath and then knocked just as I had been taught to: not too loud and not for too long.

After what seemed like forever, I heard the Reverend Mother say, 'Come.'

I turned the brass handle of the heavy door and pushed it open. She was sitting behind her huge desk, and she smiled at me. I couldn't see Daddy because he was sitting in the big chair with the high back, facing the Reverend Mother.

'You have a very special visitor, Evelyn,' she said, and motioned me forward. 'Come in and sit down.'

When I got closer to the desk and could peer around the side of the tall chair, I saw that it wasn't Daddy at all; it was Mammy. She was wearing a fur coat that looked too big for her, and she was crying quietly.

'What do you want?' I said.

I was angry with her for not being Daddy and for all the boys being in Kilkenny and for none of us being together. I wanted to leave the office, and I turned towards the door.

The Reverend Mother rose from her chair. 'Sit down, child! Where are your manners?'

I wondered if she still didn't know my name, after all this time.

Mammy reached out towards me but I stayed where I was.

Even though I didn't ask her, she said, 'I had no choice, pet, I'm sorry. When you're older, maybe you'll understand.'

Then she started crying again, more noisily now.

The Reverend Mother came round the desk and handed her a handkerchief and tried to soothe her. I stood there watching them. The Reverend Mother said she would go and get a pot of tea.

'You two must have a lot to catch up on,' she said to Mammy, and she threw me a look that meant: you'd better behave.

Mammy dried her eyes and gave me a weak little smile.

'I have something for you,' she said, and handed me a long box wrapped in brown paper.

A present! I ripped off the paper. Lying inside the box was the most beautiful doll I had ever seen. She had curly blonde hair and round blue eyes with lids that could open and close.

'She walks and talks,' Mammy said.

I stared at the doll in her box. I was nearly afraid to pick her up. Mammy lifted her out and held her by the hands and showed me how she walked. When Mammy leaned the doll towards me, the doll said, 'Ma-ma, Ma-ma.'

I was so happy, I burst into tears and threw my arms around Mammy. She held me, but she didn't say anything. I was crying and at the same time trying to think of a way to make Mammy come back to us. But the more frantically I tried, the more confused my thoughts became, and so I said nothing.

Mammy didn't stay long that afternoon; she said she

couldn't. But she was coming back the following day to visit, and the Reverend Mother had given permission for her to take me to the city. That night, I passed the new doll around among the other girls and there was great excitement. Each one gave the doll a hug and we decided we would name her Molly.

The next morning, Mother Teresa, who looked after the tailoring and sewing rooms, dressed me in a new black and yellow frock and gave me a lovely emerald-green cloak to wear over it. I felt very pretty as I sat there waiting for Mammy.

She arrived just after breakfast in a taxi that took us to the city centre of Dublin. We went shopping on O'Connell Street. In the toy department of Clery's, Mammy bought me a pair of roller skates. I was so excited I couldn't speak; I had never been in a shop full of this many toys and I thought that Santy must have been here, even though it wasn't Christmas.

The man in the shop wrapped the skates neatly in a brown paper parcel and tied the lot with pink string, and Mammy and I walked along the busy street with our parcel. Although they were wrapped up, I imagined that everyone could see my lovely new skates.

We went for a slice of cake and lemonade in Bewley's and afterwards, we got on a tram.

'We're going to see Granny in Dún Laoghaire,' Mammy said.

The day was getting better and better.

The tram stopped alongside the sea, and we walked the short distance to Granny's house. Granny hugged me and admired my green cloak and told me what a pretty girl I was. The house was full of aunties and uncles who had come to visit, and I met cousins I didn't know I had. We ate a dinner that Granny had prepared and afterwards Mammy took me for a walk by the seaside.

'Now you're not to tell Daddy that I've been to see you,' she said.

I asked her to give me her address, but she wouldn't.

'You won't need it, pet,' she said. 'I'll visit you often.'

By the time we got back on the tram to return to Dublin, it was getting dark. Mammy brought me to a restaurant in the city where all the tables were in separate booths. Inside each booth, there was a little machine on the wall. If you put money into the machine, you could choose your own music. Mammy put a few coins in and chose the *Anniversary Waltz*. The man who was singing sounded very sad. Mammy played it over and over, and she began to look sad.

After that, we headed back to the convent. By the time we got there, Mammy was her smiling, happy self again.

She said, 'I'll see you tomorrow. I'll be here around dinner time. Goodnight and God bless.'

That night when I went to bed, I knew that when Mammy came tomorrow I could convince her to stay in Dublin and we could all be together again. She'd seemed so young and happy all day, except during the *Anniversary Waltz*. I could hardly wait for tomorrow.

The next day was warm and sunny and all the girls were out playing in the field behind the convent. Everyone tried out my new skates. Because there were so many of us, we took turns wearing only one at a time, and skated as best we could like that. I heard my name being called and saw Mammy walking up the path toward the field. I left the skates and ran to meet her. She had a white box in her hands and she set it on the ground so that she could hug me.

Then she told me to pick up the box. 'I've brought wafers for everyone,' she said.

Inside was a pile of ice-cream wafers. I carried the box back to where the girls were playing and we all sat on the grass eating ice-cream. Mammy sat in the middle, telling stories about Scotland and answering questions about the latest songs in the hit parade. After a while, she told me that she had to go.

As she stood up, she said, 'Will you walk with me to the gate?'

I took her hand and, when we were a short bit away from the girls, I asked her why she was leaving.

'Don't go, Mammy, please. Come back to us and then we can all come home from the schools and be together again.'

She knelt down in front of me and told me that it was impossible. She said she couldn't live with Daddy and we couldn't be a family anymore.

'You're better off where you are,' she said.

'But, Mammy...'

She hugged me and said, 'I have to go now, pet. Mind yourself and tell the boys that I'm thinking of them. But don't tell your daddy I've been here,' she reminded me.

She stood up and turned away and walked quickly through the gate. I stood crying and watching her go, saying, 'Mammy, come back, come back,' just like I had on St Stephen's Day.

Mother Bernadette appeared out of nowhere and took me gently by the arm and led me into the convent. She tried to make me drink some warm milk but it had something disgusting in it and I was sick all over the bed. That night, I had a nightmare again, but this time Mammy was flying over the sea and my brothers were being engulfed in flames.

The nuns were especially nice to me after that and I was very popular because I had the skates and the new doll and I didn't mind sharing them.

One windy day in late September, I was helping Mother Bridget collect fruit in the orchard when Mother Imelda appeared.

'You have a special visitor,' she said, and told me to hurry along to the Reverend Mother's office.

This time, I wasn't so excited and I took my time getting there. I had got as far as the hall but was still a good distance from the office door when I heard shouting.

It was Daddy! He was home from England! And he was roaring at the Reverend Mother. He was even cursing at her.

'You feckin old bitch,' Daddy was saying, 'she's my daughter and I'm taking her.'

I stood frozen in place outside the door and held my breath. Daddy would surely go to hell for saying that.

'And there is nothing you or Jesus Christ himself can do to stop it!'

I didn't even knock this time, just burst straight in. Daddy's face was only inches from the Reverend Mother's. He had a wild look in his eyes and there was spit at the corners of his mouth. The Reverend Mother was standing straight as a poker and seemed calm as could be. They both turned to look at me. For a few seconds, nobody moved. Then Daddy ran across the office and scooped me up. I clung to his neck and started crying. I was scared but I thought that maybe all this commotion meant that I was going home.

Mother Bernadette and Mother Imelda were standing behind me; I hadn't heard them come in. The Reverend Mother said to Mother Bernadette, 'Take Evelyn to recreation.'

The two nuns tried to take me from Daddy but he was holding me tight. I didn't know what was happening but I was beginning to think it was something bad.

Daddy looked at Mother Bernadette and Mother Imelda, who had their hands on my arms. 'Brides of Christ or not,' he shouted, 'you're not having my little girl. Now feck off, you old bitches!'

Very calmly, the Reverend Mother told Daddy that, much as she would like to release me, her hands were tied.

'It's the law,' she said. 'Both you and your wife must apply to the court. Until then, the State, in this instance represented by me, have custody of all your children, including Evelyn, until they reach the age of sixteen. And if you remove Evelyn from this convent, the Gardai will pursue you and return her to us.'

Daddy was still holding onto me, staring with his wild eyes at the Reverend Mother. I was terrified for his soul because of all the cursing and I knew it was up to me to save it. I told him that I had to go to Rosary now but would be back. I wriggled free of him and, as the two nuns hustled me towards the door, I heard the Reverend Mother saying to Daddy that perhaps he should come back and visit me when he was in a better frame of mind.

That night I went to sleep feeling very happy. Daddy had come to the convent for the first time since the day he'd left me there and this surely meant that I would soon see my brothers and we would all be together again.

Daddy hadn't come back from England alone. He'd brought someone with him, a woman who would help him look after his children once he'd got us home again.

When he'd arrived in Liverpool off the boat, he'd made his way by train and bus to the address on the newspaper clipping that was still in his pocket. It was a building site in Huddersfield, north of Holmfirth. He was told he could start the following Monday. When Daddy asked the foreman if he knew of any digs in the area, the foreman told him of a Mrs Brown who ran a nice clean house in Holmfirth. The foreman didn't know the address but he told Daddy to ask at the village pub.

Daddy did as directed. He was standing at the bar when he noticed a group of old fellows playing dominoes with an attractive woman. The woman was wearing a man's coat over her shoulders. She came to the bar and ordered a round of drinks, for herself and the domino players.

Daddy told her he was looking for a Mrs Brown and asked if she had any idea where he might find her.

The woman stepped back from the bar and looked Daddy up and down, rather rudely. In a harsh and unfriendly voice, she said, 'Who wants to know?'

Daddy told her he did. He was looking for clean digs and

the foreman at his new job had recommended a Mrs Brown.

'Would you know where I could find her?' he asked again.

The woman continued to stare at Daddy. Finally, she said, 'I'm Mrs Brown and I do have digs, but I don't like the Irish. You drink too much and you cause trouble.'

But with all of her staring, she'd noticed his clean clothes and polished shoes.

'However,' she said, 'I'll give you a chance. I charge two pound, ten shillings a week for bed and breakfast, four pound a week all in. And I take two weeks in advance.'

Daddy moved in that night.

Daddy had been lodging with Mrs Brown – or Jessie, as he called her by then – for more than six weeks, and she knew next to nothing about him. Years later he told me a lot about this time. He was clean, he left the house every morning at six o'clock sharp, and he paid his rent every Friday when he came home from work. He had no women friends that she knew of, but he went to the pub every night for a couple of hours, played the piano and drank a few pints. The women in the village ribbed her about him. They all said he was handsome and mysterious.

One night, when Jessie was passing Daddy's room, she heard muffled sobs. She stood outside the door for a minute, not knowing whether to knock or pretend she hadn't heard. She decided to go back to bed but lay awake most of the night. She thought maybe Daddy'd had bad news from home because she had only ever seen him laughing and joking and acting like he hadn't a care in the world.

The following day was Donkey Stone Day, when all the women in the street could be found on their knees, scrubbing their front steps. They wore wraparound flowered aprons, scarves tied like turbans, and furry ankle boots. As they scrubbed, they gossiped amongst themselves and gave out about their husbands. Jessie herself was married to a man named David who drank too much and seldom had work. He spent most of his time in the pub. When he was home, Daddy'd taken care to avoid him.

Jessie was doing her own steps when she heard Daddy's voice behind her.

'You could say one for me when you're down there,' he said.

Jessie stood up. He sounded his old happy self again, and she felt a little flustered, thinking about last night and how she'd heard him crying in his bedroom.

'What brings you back at this time of day?' she asked. 'Sacked you, have they?'

She sloshed the yellow water over the pavement, accidentally wetting Daddy's shoes. Daddy said he wanted to talk to her and she said, 'All right. I'll put the kettle on. But mind you wipe your feet. I've just swilled the hall.'

Daddy thought her expressions were funny. 'Swill', where he came from, was what you gave to pigs. Jessie prepared a tea tray and took off her dirty apron and her wet boots and joined Daddy in the sitting room.

Daddy's face grew serious. He told her he had to go to Ireland for a couple of weeks, and he asked her would she keep the room for him.

'Of course I'll keep the room for you, Dessie.'

She couldn't come right out and ask him what the

trouble was; she didn't want to seem nosy. And she certainly didn't mention anything about the previous night and standing outside his door. But she did say, 'Has something happened? You looked a little pale this morning.'

Daddy was silent for a few minutes.

When he spoke, he said, 'Jessie, I have six children in Ireland, and I miss them desperately. They're locked up in schools because their feckin mother has deserted us. I need someone to look after them.'

Jessie knew then why he'd been crying, and her heart went out to him, but she didn't see how she could help.

Daddy continued. He told her how fond he'd grown of her. Then he said, 'You've no life here with that lazy, drunken gobshite. Would you think about coming to Ireland with me?'

Jessie was shocked, but she gave nothing away. She'd thought about leaving David more than once and maybe this was her chance. Daddy seemed kind and gentle and he was always full of fun. But she was ten years older than he was, and how would she manage with six children?

'We'll talk properly when you get back from Dublin,' was all she said.

Daddy tried to get something a little more promising from Jessie, but she wouldn't be drawn. She just kept saying, 'We'll talk when you get back.'

Daddy decided not to go to Dublin, not for the time being, anyway. He was encouraged, even by Jessie's uncertainty, and he stayed put to try to persuade her.

Weeks passed. Daddy went to work and Jessie carried on with her own duties. Daddy's invitation hung in the air between them. One day, Daddy was on his way home from work. It was raining and a bitterly cold wind was sweeping through the Pennines. The foreman at Daddy's job had sent all the men home early. The job was nearly at an end by then.

Daddy got off the bus in Holmfirth and saw Jessie struggling up the street with two heavy bags of shopping. He caught up with her and took the bags and they walked home in silence together. Daddy followed her into the small back kitchen and watched as she unpacked the shopping. He lit two cigarettes and passed one to her. He said he was definitely going back to Ireland when the job was finished. Then he told Jessie that he'd fallen in love with her.

'Come with me,' he said.

When Jessie finally responded, her voice was so low, Daddy couldn't be sure what she'd said. He looked at her and asked again.

She walked towards him and said, more confidently now, 'All right then. All right, I'll come with you.'

Daddy was over the moon. He scooped her up in his arms and twirled her about the little kitchen and promised her she'd never regret it.

Before they went anywhere, they had to deal with David. Daddy told Jessie that he would be right there beside her when she told him. David was a slight man, but he could be violent if provoked.

When David came home from the pub that evening, Jessie announced her plan. She hardly had the words out before her husband lunged at her and knocked her to the floor, shouting, 'You bloody slut.'

David's reaction had been so swift, Daddy hadn't even

had time to step in, but now his fist connected with David's nose. Blood poured down David's face, and he staggered backwards and fell into his chair. Jessie ran to the kitchen to get a towel.

'If you ever touch her again,' Daddy said, 'I'll kill you.'

David snatched the towel from Jessie. Wiping the blood from his face, he pleaded with her not to go.

'Give me another chance, love,' he said. 'Things will be different, I swear.'

Jessie looked at Daddy, begging him for guidance, but Daddy couldn't help her. This had to be her decision. For a moment, nobody said anything. Daddy lit a cigarette and stared out the window, smoking and listening to the old clock ticking noisily on the mantle. David thought Jessie's hesitation meant that she might be changing her mind. Rising from his chair, he shook the bloodied towel at Daddy and shouted, 'Get out of my house, you dirty Irish pig! Go on, get out! She's my wife and she's staying here with me.'

He moved to Jessie's side and put an arm around her shoulder, possessively. The stench of blood and stale alcohol was too much for Jessie. It reminded her of what life with David had been like, and she knew that if she stayed with him, the rest of her life would be more of the same. She pulled away from him and went over to Daddy.

'It's over,' she said to David. 'I'm sorry, but it's over.'

Jessie fled the room and went to pack her meagre belongings.

FOUR

Daddy and Jessie moved into Granddad's four-room house on Innisfallen Parade, and Daddy started straight away on the job of getting his children back. He wrote to the Minister for Education himself, explaining that he had returned to Ireland with a housekeeper and that they were living with his father. He told the Minister that he had been prevented from taking his daughter out of the convent and bringing her home to live with him. '...so I would be obliged if you would be kind enough to order the release of my daughter at once,' he wrote.

He knew that when the Minister gave the order for me, the boys would be released too. He signed the letter 'Desmond Doyle Esq.' and dropped it in the post, certain he'd have us home in no time at all.

When Daddy came to the convent again to see me, he brought Jessie with him. He called her Jessie when he spoke to her but to me he said, 'Evelyn, this is your new mammy.'

I smiled sweetly at the new mammy, then ignored her for the rest of the visit.

Daddy took us to the Strawberry Beds, the area west of Dublin along the Liffey, where he'd grown up. When Daddy was a boy, he'd fished the river there, gone rabbiting to earn a few pennies and picked wild gypsophila with his best friend Gussie Hair-oil. Gussie and Daddy sold the gypsophila to the flower-barrow ladies who came through the village on their way to set up their stalls in the Dublin markets.

We walked along the banks of the Liffey. I was skipping ahead when I turned around and saw Daddy and Jessie holding hands. I stopped skipping and felt anger rising in me. Even if our old mammy was gone, we didn't need a new mammy. Especially not one with a funny English accent who called me 'love' and 'cocker'. What was Daddy thinking? I ran back and forced my way between them. Jessie offered me her hand and I brushed it aside. I made sure that the two of them did not get too close to each other for the rest of the afternoon.

When we got back to the convent, Daddy said goodbye and promised that he would come and take me home the following week. I cried and said I wanted to go right now.

'We have to wait for the Minister,' he said.

I asked him who the Minister was.

'The Minister is the man who is going to sign the papers so that you and the boys can come home. So be patient and be a good girl for the nuns.'

But Daddy didn't take me home the next week or even the week after that. The Minister was a very busy man and had not yet replied to Daddy's letter.

Three weeks later, an envelope with the government stamp on it arrived at Granddad's house. Daddy tore it open, expecting to find our release papers. Instead, it contained a letter telling him that he could not take me out of the convent.

He read it out to Jessie and Granddad. 'It says here that I must "furnish proof of suitable accommodation and suitable female assistance" and that bringing Evelyn home now "would not be in the child's best interests." Not in the child's best interests! Now what the feck does that mean? Who does he think he is, anyway, and how does he know what's best for my child?'

Daddy ranted on that way stomping around the sitting room in Granddad's house. Jessie had never seen Daddy so angry, not even during the scene with David before they'd left England. Granddad let him vent himself. When Daddy's rage was finally spent, Granddad put a hand on his shoulder and gently forced him into a chair.

'Tomorrow,' he said, 'we'll go see my solicitor.' Then he nodded towards Jessie, who was cowering in a corner, and went off to his own room to play the cello.

The following day, Daddy and Granddad brought the Minister's letter to Michael Beatty, Granddad's solicitor. Mr Beatty was a specialist in family law, though he had never married or had a family himself. He was devoted only to his work.

He frowned as he read the letter, then turned to Daddy and said, 'It would appear, Desmond, that someone has misinformed the Minister by advising him to ask you for proof of suitable accommodation and female assistance. Because even if you were to provide such proof, he still would not be able to consider your application for Evelyn's release.'

'And why is that?' Daddy asked.

'The consent of both parents, that's you *and* your wife, is required in order for your children to be released. It's there in the Children Act of 1941, Section 10. This section authorises a judge to send a child to an industrial school who is destitute but not an orphan if her parents are unable to support her. The judge can dispense with one of the parent's consent when he's ordering the committal, as happened in your case. But when an application arises for the same child's release from the school, the consent of both parents is required.'

It was the same thing that the Reverend Mother had told him, and Daddy hated hearing that he would need Mammy to get me released.

'Let me write to the Minister,' Mr Beatty said. 'I'll tell him what's happened and I will emphasize your distress at being separated from your children. Now, let's talk about your circumstances.'

Daddy explained that he had got work with the Dublin Corporation and was earning £8 7s 6d a week. Jessie was his housekeeper, and he gave her board plus £2 a week.

Mr Beatty took notes, then told Daddy to go straight to the Housing Department.

'Apply to the Corporation for a house. Your father's won't be near big enough if all those children come home.'

Daddy found the Allocations Section at the Housing Department and took a seat on one of the long wooden benches in the waiting area. The room was full of women and screaming children, all smelling like they hadn't washed in ages. Posters on the walls showed magnified fleas and other insects Daddy'd never even heard of. The posters were full of information about the deadly benefits of DDT. The mothers and children on the benches were all in a queue and, every so often, Daddy would get up and shuffle to the next bench. After about two hours of inching along, he heard a bored-sounding voice say, 'Next,' and it was his turn.

Daddy approached the desk. He was embarrassed that everyone in the room could listen to his personal business, so he spoke as quietly as he could, explaining to the man about how his children were coming home and wouldn't all fit in their Granddad's house.

'Speak up!' the clerk said, without looking up from the papers on his desk.

Daddy was already in bad humour. Because of the wait, he'd lost half a day's work. Now the man's attitude was annoying him even more.

'I need a house so I can get my children out of the schools,' he said, gritting his teeth.

The man didn't react, he didn't even look up. He just pushed a green form across the desk and kept scribbling on his notepad. Daddy started to fill in the form right there at the clerk's desk.

'And I want one with a garden,' he added.

This got the clerk's attention. He removed his glasses and looked squarely at Daddy.

'Mr Doyle,' he said, 'your present accommodation appears adequate to your immediate needs.' He nodded towards the others still waiting on the benches. 'Some of these people are living ten to a room. So unless there are health grounds for your claim, you will have a long wait. Now, go away and fill in that form and return it to this office when you've finished. We'll let you know when something comes up.'

'How long is the waiting list?' Daddy asked, angrier now. He'd lost half a day's wages for nothing.

'Mr Doyle, I don't make the rules. If you're not happy, write to the bloody Taoiseach!' And he peered around the side of Daddy and said, 'Next.'

'Dear Mr Costello, I want a nice house in Dollymount for my six children and my lovely "housekeeper", and I want you to pay the rent as well.'

Daddy and Granddad and Jessie fell about the place laughing when Daddy told them about the clerk at the Housing Department.

'Imagine,' Daddy said, 'the feckin Taoiseach.'

They laughed till their sides ached and then they all went to the pub and forgot about everything that troubled them.

In November, Mr Beatty asked Daddy to come to his office. He had received a response from the Minister. Daddy sat nervously turning his hat in his hands as he watched the solicitor sifting through the piles of paper on his desk. At last, Mr Beatty extracted the letter from the chaos he called his filing system.

'Well, Desmond,' he said, 'I'm afraid it's not good news.'

He started to read the letter aloud to Daddy. It was full of 'considerations' and 'regrets' and 'circumstances'. Daddy became impatient.

'Give it to me in plain English, will you?' he demanded.

Mr Beatty handed him the letter.

> *It is regretted that your application to have further con-*
> *sideration given to the question of the child's discharge*
> *cannot, therefore, be granted.*

The Minister had simply repeated what he'd said in his first letter, referring to the 'child's best interests' and suggesting that if Daddy were to furnish 'satisfactory evidence' of suitable accommodation and female assistance, the matter would be further considered.

Daddy crumpled the letter and threw it down on Mr Beatty's desk. Without saying a word, he walked out of the office.

Less than a week later, Daddy and Mr Beatty were sitting in the waiting room outside the office of TJ Conolly, one of the most senior barristers in Dublin. Mr Conolly had heard about Daddy from Nick Barron. Nick was an old friend of Mr Beatty's who'd spent the last several years working as an attorney in America. Now Nick was back in Dublin practising family law. He'd brought his two children home with him, but not his wife; a 'housekeeper' was looking after the children. The other men teased him about his rather attractive housekeeper, but Nick didn't seem to mind.

The previous day, Nick had bumped into Mr Beatty by chance outside the Four Courts, the centre of legal business in Ireland. Mr Beatty was there pleading a case for 'Red' Maloney, or Rosemary Eileen Dolores Maloney, who'd been a client of his since her first arrest for soliciting at the age of seventeen. That was only a few years ago, but already Red had grown haggard and looked almost twice her age. Mr Beatty half wished that, for her own sake, the justices would give Red a long gaol sentence rather than another short spell in High Park Penitentiary.

As Nick and Mr Beatty had stood on the steps of the Four Courts chatting, Mr Beatty had mentioned Daddy's problem to Nick. Nick had taken an interest immediately; he had a reputation for taking on the most difficult cases. Mr Beatty showed him the Minister's letter, and Nick took it straight to Mr Conolly in the barristers' chambers.

Sometimes Mr Conolly found Nick's enthusiasm for lost causes a bit tiresome, but he read the letter anyway, and said: 'Jaysus, I believe I will have a look at this. Have Beatty and Doyle in my office tomorrow after court adjourns.'

Daddy and Mr Beatty sat waiting outside Mr Conolly's office. The walls in the room were wood-panelled and hung with oil paintings of solemn and important-looking men. Magazines about fly fishing and game shooting were neatly displayed on a large, round coffee table. A dozen chairs made of rich burgundy leather were arranged in clusters. There was a thick Persian carpet and a fire blazing in the fireplace. An immaculately dressed secretary eyed Daddy disapprovingly.

'Whatever happens, Desmond,' Mr Beatty said quietly, 'don't lose your temper. If TJ takes you on, you can be sure he'll do everything possible. It might take some time, but you couldn't have a better advocate.'

At last, the secretary told them that Mr Conolly was ready to see them, and she led them up a grand wide staircase to the office.

Mr Conolly was huge and slightly unkempt. He was known in legal circles as a 'loose cannon'. He might've made the bench as a justice, if he hadn't scuppered his own chances by not playing the political game. He gruffly launched straight into the business at hand.

'It would seem,' Mr Conolly said, 'that our friend the Minister, Mr Mulcahy, has his own interpretation of the conditions whereby he could release Evelyn. His letter ignores the actual criteria which would enable him to do so. That is,' he said, looking at Daddy, 'an application for Evelyn's release signed by both you and your wife.'

He had a thick law book opened before him. Smoothed out alongside it was the letter from the Minister that Daddy had crumpled up and thrown on Mr Beatty's desk.

Mr Conolly continued. 'You earn more than £8 a week and you share your father's house on Innisfallen Parade. Here's what we'll do. We will apply for an order of *mandamus*. That should get the Minister's attention.'

Daddy looked at Mr Beatty, but Mr Beatty held up his hand to silence Daddy. 'This is going to be a lengthy process,' Mr Conolly said. 'I'm sorry, Mr Doyle, but there's not much chance of having your children home by Christmas. I'll let you know when the hearing will be.'

He stood up to indicate that the meeting was over. Daddy had expected more promising news from such an important man.

When they were back out on the street, Daddy said to Mr Beatty, 'I promised Evelyn she'd be home for Christmas. And what the feck is *mandamus*, anyway?'

'An order of *mandamus*,' Mr Beatty explained, 'means that the court orders someone to do what they're supposed to do. In this case, they'll order the government to perform its legal and lawful duties. The Minister will be forced to explain why he won't consider your application for Evelyn's release. But,' he added, 'you have to understand. When Mulcahy's office gets this order slapped on them, they'll have the very best counsel and they'll see straight away what the actual criteria is: you need your wife's signature.'

'But she's gone!'

Mr Beatty shook his head. 'I can't see any other way of getting the children home.'

It was nearly a year since Mammy had gone away.

The convent was buzzing with activity as we all prepared for Christmas. There was a nativity grotto set up in the main entrance hall. The statues were life-sized, and the lights hidden behind them made them look as if they could come to life at any minute.

All the girls were getting new cloaks because Alfie Byrne, the Lord Mayor, was taking the industrial schools from all over Ireland to the Gaiety Theatre to watch the last dress rehearsals of the Christmas pantomime. I was helping Mother Teresa in the sewing room to write out name tags and put them on the new cloaks when the telephone rang in her office.

It was a message for me to come to the Reverend Mother's office because Daddy was there. As I hurried down the long hallway, I was sure that he'd come to take me home, but as soon as I opened the door, I knew something was wrong. He didn't even smile when he saw me.

'Daddy,' I said, 'are we going home for Christmas?'

'I'm sorry pet,' he said, 'I can't take you home just yet.'

For the first time in months, I cried. I clung to him and he tried to comfort me. He told me he would fight to his last breath to get me and the boys home. But for now, he explained, the government wouldn't let me out, not even for Christmas. The big lump came back in my chest. Daddy told me to be a brave girl.

'I'll come as often as I can,' he said, 'and after Christmas, I'll take you to see the boys in Kilkenny.'

Back at Granddad's house, Daddy told Granddad and Jessie about his new plan, in case the Minister decided not to release us.

'When I get Evelyn out to see the boys in the new year,' he said, 'I'll take her and the three eldest in the car, and we'll go to Belfast. We'll be gone before they even miss us. Then, when we're settled, I'll come back for the babies.'

Granddad stared at him. 'You can't be serious! You may get the four of them out of the Free State all right, but you wouldn't be able to set foot back in this country. And your chances of ever seeing the babies again would be nil.'

Daddy thought for a moment. 'Well,' he said, '*you* could get the babies.'

Granddad smoked his Sweet Afton and said nothing for a while. Finally, he spoke in the slow and deliberate way that could drive Daddy mad.

'Here's what we'll do,' he said. 'I'll take Evelyn to Belfast after Christmas while you carry on with the solicitors. If and when the commotion dies down, you can go and get the boys.'

Granddad had never been out of Ireland and he hated all things English. But if this was the way it had to be so be it.

The day of the Christmas pantomime, we wore our new green cloaks. There were special buses lined up in convoy to take us to the theatre, and we felt very important. Before we got on the bus, Mother Bernadette gave us a lecture about good behaviour and showing the public that we were 'young ladies'. We cheered and roared right through her speech, but she shouted over us.

'We will get off the buses some distance from the theatre. So you must stay together, girls, and be smart about it.'

She clapped her hands twice, and we formed a long queue down the footpath. People on the street stopped to watch the orphans on their day out, and we waved at them as we boarded.

We rode across the river and up to St Stephen's Green, where there were even more buses with more children on them. I had never seen so many buses; they were parked all around the Green, and there were still more pulling up. We got off our bus and Mother Bernadette lined us all up in twos, counted our heads and told us to follow her.

'And keep together, girls,' she called.

She set off at a brisk pace with a double crocodile of green-cloaked girls following behind. I was still amazed by all the buses and was watching them as they passed. Out of the corner of my eye, I caught a glimpse of something moving in the back windows of one. I ran a bit ahead to see what it was and there, waving wildly at me, were Noel and Maurice! They were on their way to the pantomime too. I ran alongside their bus but as it turned onto the north side of the green, Mother Bernadette caught me and told me to get back in line.

When we got inside the Gaiety Theatre, we were all given candy-striped paper bags tied with coloured string.

The bags were full of sweets and fruit. A lady in a dark red dress with gold bits on the shoulders led us to our seats. She was wearing a hat shaped like a boat and the hat had bits of gold on it too. I decided then and there that I wanted to work at the theatre so I could wear a beautiful outfit like hers. She led us down what seemed like hundreds of tiny steps and pointed to an empty block of seats in the middle. I sat next to the aisle so that I could see my brothers when they came in.

When the lights went down and the orchestra struck up, I crept out of my seat. It took a minute for my eyes to get adjusted to the dark but, when they did, all I could see were large blocks of colour: grey and red and blue and black and every shade of green you could think of. I couldn't remember what colour my brothers were wearing. I made many trips to the lav, taking a different route each time, thinking I might see the boys, but I never did. Finally, I gave up and sat in the foyer crying and missed the whole show.

All the girls at the convent were allowed to go to midnight Mass on Christmas Eve. When the nuns sang hymns on their own, it was lovely and I felt sad. Christmas Day, a show band came to the convent and we all joined in a singsong. We sang, 'She wore red ribbons and a hula-hula skirt'. I thought a hula-hula skirt must be a wonderful thing, but I couldn't imagine what one would look like.

We had a dinner of chicken and sausages and Christmas pudding and custard. We ate so much that the nuns made us go outside afterwards and play running games. Daddy and Granddad came to visit that night and brought me a dolls' tea set and a stove that could be lit with spirit and cotton wadding. The nuns asked Daddy to keep the stove at home for me in case I burned the place down. Daddy told me that the court hearing would be in a couple of weeks and that I might be able to come home after that. But in any case, he said, we were going to visit the boys in Kilkenny after the new year.

Granny didn't come to see me that Christmas. I never saw her again.

Toward the end of January, Daddy and his counsel appeared in the High Court for the *mandamus* hearing.

The application for my release based on Daddy's income and housing situation was ruled invalid and the justices determined, therefore, that the Minister had not failed in his duties. Daddy's counsel knew the application was invalid, because the criteria the Minister had asked him to fulfil were irrelevant to my release, but they wanted this acknowledged in court. They needed to get the case off the ground by establishing the real condition Daddy needed to fulfil.

Now Mr Conolly began arguing with the three judges about the section of the Children Act that required the consent of 'the parents' in order for the Minister to discharge a child from an industrial school. He pointed out that the Interpretation Act provided that 'every word importing the plural shall, unless the contrary intention appears, be construed as if it also imported the singular.' In this case, he argued, it provided for the substitution of 'parent' for 'parents'. Mr Conolly could see what the outcome of the hearing was going to be, but he was enjoying the fight anyway.

Daddy abruptly left his seat and stomped out of the courtroom. He was pacing up and down the foyer, pulling hard on a cigarette, when Mr Beatty joined him.

'Desmond, you will have to watch that temper of yours, or you'll find yourself in trouble with the court and we'll lose the services of the best team in the country.'

'It would help if I knew what was going on,' Daddy said.

'Well,' Mr Beatty said, 'the Minister's counsel have said that your income and accommodation are irrelevant.'

Daddy was exasperated. 'Then why did they keep asking me for it?'

'The only thing that matters, as far as they're concerned, is that you have your wife's permission and signature if you want to get your children back. Unless, of course, your wife is dead.'

Daddy was sick of hearing about Mammy and her signature; it was beginning to sound like a broken record. Mr Beatty looked sideways at him. He knew Daddy well enough by now to know what was going through his mind. He smiled to himself; he liked Daddy and admired his determination.

Shortly, Mr Conolly and Nick joined them in the foyer. Mr Conolly was beaming and rubbing his hands together.

'We lost, didn't we?' Daddy asked. 'So what the feck are you grinning at?'

Daddy wasn't just thinking about the fact that they'd lost; he was also thinking about how much all of this was going to cost. These people spent as much on a fancy meal as he earned in a week. Granddad had offered to put up the money for the legal bills, but Daddy didn't know how much Granddad could afford. And anyway, they might need all the money they could get their hands on if they were going to spirit us out of the country.

'We needed to have them state in court exactly what they wanted from you,' Mr Conolly said. 'Now that they have, we can properly prepare our case.'

He clapped Daddy on the back.

'Come on, Desmond,' he said, 'cheer up. We've rattled them not a little, I suspect. Now will you join us for a glass?'

Jessie was on her way out of Granddad's one morning when she met a man just about to knock on the door. He tipped his hat.

'Ah! Good morning, Miss. Would you spare a few minutes for a survey?'

Jessie let him in, thinking he must be from the census bureau. He asked her questions about the house and about who was living there. He was pleasant and full of jokes. She even thought he was flirting with her a little – most of the men she'd met in Dublin were charmers – and she was grateful for the attention. They chatted away over a pot of tea.

As the man drained the last of the tea from his cup and stood to go, he said casually, 'So I take it you're all of the faith?'

'Well,' Jessie said, 'I'm C of E, actually.'

It seemed an innocent enough question and, for the time being, she thought no more about it.

Jessie was finding it hard to settle in to her new life in Dublin. Daddy was putting in long hours for the Corporation and, more often than not, would go for a pint after work. Jessie had tried to find work herself, but her English accent put people off and eventually, she gave up. She prayed that Daddy would get his children home soon so that she would feel useful again. With only three rooms to clean and just Daddy and Granddad to look after, her days dragged by. Mostly she spent her time wandering through the shops and the markets. At home, she hesitated to play the wireless in case it would disturb Granddad and bring on one of his headaches. When Granddad got a headache, he would wander about the house with a dirty sock wrapped around his head. He insisted that the sweat from the sock, being so strong, was the only effective way of curing the pain.

Often, Jessie didn't find Granddad easy to get on with. There was only so much housework he would tolerate, and he'd get tetchy with her if she fussed too much, sweeping and polishing and scrubbing. He'd lived alone for years and had his own ways, and he wanted nothing so much as a quiet routine. He had suffered the indignities of communal living once already when, years ago, he'd found himself living in a second-floor tenement flat on the North Circular Road. He'd shared a sink with the women on the third floor and its tap dripped constantly, just outside his door. Granddad got up early one morning and removed the tap and bent the lead pipe with his pliers, cutting off the supply and forcing the women to trudge to the bottom landing for water. They roared at him as they passed his door each day, but their complaints were nothing compared to the dripping tap. As for the shared toilet, Granddad had refused even to consider it. He used a milk bottle instead, in the privacy of his own flat, and went to the local pub for anything more serious.

After three years of that, Granddad had managed to buy the house on Innisfallen Parade. By that time, he was the lead cellist at the Gate Theatre. He earned extra money doing occasional painting and decorating jobs, where he would often find himself working alongside Daddy. They were both on a job at Dublin Castle the day Brendan Behan tried to shoot Daddy.

Daddy was the foreman and his men were painting St Patrick's Hall, the centrepiece of the state apartments at the Castle. They had set up their ladders and placed planks of wood about a foot wide between each ladder, for walking on. That morning, Brendan didn't show up for work till after ten and, even by his standards, he was paralytic drunk. Under normal circumstances, Daddy would have sent him off to gloss skirting boards – a certain amount of drinking, after all, was accepted practice in the building trade – but that day was different. They were all working six or seven feet up and a pot of gloss on the expensive carpet would have meant the whole lot of them getting sacked. Daddy told Brendan to go home for the day and come back in the morning when he was sober.

'Are you accusing me of being fughing drunk?' Brendan asked.

Daddy said, 'That's right, you're fughing drunk. Now, go home.'

'Make me,' Brendan said.

Daddy didn't have time for this; painters earned their wages by being fast and clean.

'You can just get your cards then,' he told Brendan.

Brendan wanted to fight but the other men restrained

him and convinced him to go peacefully.

The following day, as the men sat in the back courtyard having their midday sandwiches, Brendan appeared, slightly unsteady on his feet and waving a hand pistol.

'C'mere, Doyle,' he shouted, 'I'm going to shoot you. You're worth the price of a bullet.'

Daddy dropped his tomato and onion sandwich and fled. Years later, when Brendan was famous as a writer and Daddy would see him on television, he'd say, 'There's the bastard that tried to shoot me when I sacked him.'

Daddy and Jessie arrived at the convent early one morning in February to take me to Kilkenny to see the boys. Daddy had brought them each a football and Jessie had packed a picnic and we were all going to have a great day together.

As we walked out to the car, Daddy said, 'You can sit in the back, pet. Your mammy will sit beside me in the front.'

I was furious. I always sat beside Daddy in the front. All the way to Kilkenny, I hardly said a word.

My brothers' convent was in the countryside and it was lovely and peaceful there. Daddy went inside to collect the five boys, leaving me alone with Jessie inside a big glass porch. We didn't say much, and I sat there wondering how my brothers and I could get our real mammy back and make Jessie go away to England.

When my brothers appeared on the porch, I hardly knew them, they'd grown so much. They were all dressed in short grey trousers and wore ties and clean white shirts, long grey socks and sturdy boots. The three oldest boys had developed country accents and Kevin and Dermot had gone blond. They ran to greet me but the two youngest hid behind Daddy's legs. It had been just over a year since the babies had seen me, and they didn't recognize me now. Daddy took the four older boys out to play on the lawn at the front of the convent and left Dermot with Jessie and me. I immediately took him up on my knee and kept him close to me; I didn't want him to sit with Jessie.

I was bouncing Dermot on my knee when a large dead butterfly dropped from the roof of the porch. Dermot screamed, and he kept screaming until a nun came running from inside and scooped him up off my knee. He stopped crying at once and clung to her. I looked at the nun holding Dermot and I felt jealous and sad. I had always been the one my brothers came to when they were hurt or in trouble. Our lives had changed for good and it frightened me.

Daddy and the boys played football and I joined in for a bit while Jessie stayed on the porch with the nun and Dermot. Then we had our picnic and told each other what life was like in the convents. My brothers seemed happy where they were. They all agreed that their favourite nun was Sister Imelda, and I told them that I had a Mother Imelda. Daddy didn't say much, just watched us being together and talking about the nuns and our new friends and what we ate for dinner. When it was time to go, Noel and Maurice managed not to cry. John's chin wobbled, but he didn't cry either. The babies were glad to be back with the nuns.

I howled most of the way home to Dublin. That night, I prayed for all of us to be together again. I even made sure I was lying on my back with my arms folded across my chest, so the devil would not be tempted.

Daddy came to see me as often as he could. Sometimes the nuns allowed me to go out for the day with him. He didn't always bring Jessie, and the days I had him to myself were the best of all. Granny didn't visit any more because Daddy had forbidden her to, but every month, she sent me the packets of tea and the green ribbons for my hair. She always included a cheerful letter and the nuns let me write back to her. I didn't tell Daddy about Granny's parcels and letters. I knew better.

At the end of that month, one of the nuns died. Her name was Mother Ignatius. The convent went very quiet and everyone spoke in hushed tones. The silence was eerie. One night, I imagined I saw Mother Ignatius gliding through the dormitory. The Bishop came to say a requiem Mass and, afterwards, we all went to the little cemetery behind the chapel and walked round Mother Ignatius' grave in a circle, praying silently, our rosary beads draped over our hands. I wasn't praying for Mother Ignatius, though; I didn't know her. She had retired before I arrived and then she was sick in the infirmary. Instead, I prayed that Daddy would make the Minster let me come home. When we were all standing still in a circle round the grave, I caught the Bishop's eye and quickly changed my prayers. I prayed for the soul of poor saintly Mother Ignatius and directed my eyes towards heaven, in an attempt to look saintly myself.

I still missed my brothers and sometimes Mammy, too, but I didn't get the nightmares much any more and was already starting to forget what life in the flats had been like. I had friends at the convent and clean clothes and my hair was always shiny. I was the only girl with long hair. Daddy had forbidden the nuns to cut it, that first day he'd brought me to the convent, and they hadn't. The girls in my dormitory took turns brushing it and finding different ways to tie in my ribbons. I loved the attention. I had even got the hang of fixing the long brown stockings with the garters. In the beginning, they had fallen down and flapped around my ankles as we walked to school.

We didn't get hugs and kisses at the convent, but we felt loved and as though we were part of a family. We talked about our real families and how our mammies and daddies were going to take us home one day. We all looked forward to the evenings in the sewing room when Mother Teresa taught us to knit socks with four needles, casting on to two, then adding the others so that we could make a cylinder of wool. She told us stories about when she was a young girl in Connemara. She had rosy cheeks and very blue eyes and I imagined her in a whitewashed farmhouse, baking bread and making strawberry jam. I loved most of the nuns, but Mother Teresa was my favourite. The nuns sometimes punished us. If one of us did something wrong and no one owned up, we were all made to stand in a line while our legs were whacked with the strap. Mother Bernadette was our favourite strapper because she didn't whack as hard as the others and seemed to suffer more than we did. As for men, they didn't figure much in our lives at the convent, apart from the priests who took confessions and said Mass, and Old Joe, the handyman.

Old Joe went between the convent, the women's penitentiary and the mental asylum, ferrying things back and forth and fixing what he could. The girls in the convent did the laundry and our farm supplied all three of the institutions with eggs and milk and butter. In the penitentiary, they baked coconut and jam squares and other cakes, and Old Joe always made sure to bring us some in his big laundry basket, which he wheeled past our playing field on Saturday mornings.

One morning, when Jessie and Daddy came to take me out for the day, Old Joe was pushing his basket along the drive. I broke away from Daddy and rushed to catch up with Old Joe. I took his hand and pulled him over to Daddy to say hello. I was very proud that my daddy came to visit me each week and I loved to introduce him to everyone. Old Joe took off his hat and shook hands with Daddy and Jessie. When he left us to carry on with his work, Jessie muttered something to Daddy about him. I didn't understand what it was but I knew it was nasty. I got very cross and shouted at her and told her to go back to England.

'You're not my real mammy, anyway,' I said, 'and I don't like you!'

Daddy pulled me by the arm and told me to say sorry to my new mammy.

'No!' I shouted. 'I want her to go away, I don't like her!'

I was sobbing now, mostly because Daddy was annoyed with me but also because, when I looked at Jessie, something in her eyes made me think she would win.

'If you don't say sorry to your mammy,' Daddy said, 'then you can't come out with us today.' He gave me a shove in Jessie's direction.

I ran past her up the drive and into the convent and

raced up the stairs to the dormitory. I flopped face down on my bed. I didn't care if the devil was tempted. After a while, Mother Bernadette came into the dormitory and stood over me. She told me that Daddy was waiting for me downstairs.

'C'mon,' she said, 'let's wash our face, and we'll go together and say sorry to your new mammy.'

I wondered why on earth she wanted to wash her face and say sorry to Jessie. I refused to go. I was too ashamed to see Daddy, and I knew that I would not be able to tell Jessie I was sorry. But Mother Bernadette wouldn't leave until I gave in.

Daddy was sitting alone in the visiting room. He didn't look annoyed with me any more. I ran to him and he gave me a big hug. Then he said, 'We have to have a serious talk, pet.'

But we didn't have our serious talk that day. We went to the pictures instead and saw a film with Roy Rogers, Daddy's favourite singing cowboy. We each had a Choc-ice at the interval and ate sweets during the film. Jessie had vanished and I knew then that Daddy would be sending her back to England. It had turned into a perfect day.

For the next few weeks, Daddy came to see me on his own and didn't mention Jessie. I began to believe that she really had gone back to England. She wasn't even at Granddad's house when Daddy took me for a visit. We sat listening to Granddad playing music, and I sang 'Ave Maria' and wondered why it couldn't be like this all the time.

One morning in March, Daddy was to call for me at nine.

Mother Teresa was fussing something awful to get me ready, making me as smart as she could. After much tucking in and straightening and pleading with me to 'stand still, child', she stood back and eyed me up and down. Satisfied, she took me by the hand and led me to the Reverend Mother's office. Daddy was there, looking very serious. The Reverend Mother smiled at me from behind her desk. When she stood up, she towered over everything and reminded me of a giant. I stood in front of the desk with my hands behind my back, trying to imagine what had happened or, worse, what was about to happen.

'Sit down, Evelyn, child. Your father and I want to talk to you.'

I couldn't remember her ever having used my name before and I wondered was that a good sign or a bad one. I sat down and Daddy blew out a big breath.

'Ebbs, pet,' he said, 'we have to talk about your new mammy.'

I stared at him. Wasn't Jessie in England yet?

'She has agreed to leave her home and friends and family just to look after us and without her, I can't get you or the boys home. You just have to accept that, do you understand?'

I couldn't look at Daddy or the Reverend Mother. I felt sick.

'Why can't we have our real mammy back?' I asked.

Daddy said that he didn't know where she was but that, in any case, she wasn't coming home.

'She has a new life now, pet, and I couldn't live with her again.' And then, just like Mammy had, he said, 'You'll understand when you grow up.'

But I felt grown up. I knew what I wanted and it wasn't a strange English lady for a mammy, and I was sure that the boys would feel the same. The Reverend Mother came round the side of her desk. She knelt in front of me and held both my hands in hers. The Reverend Mother had never touched me before. Her hands were cool, and I was surprised to feel comforted by them.

'Evelyn, child,' she said, 'you must give this lady a chance. Our Lord says we must be charitable and kind. And you would be helping your daddy as well.'

She stood up and patted my head and then left me alone with Daddy. I didn't rush over to him like I normally would but stayed in my chair. Something in his manner or in his eyes was different today, and I thought maybe he had decided he didn't love me any more. I wondered if I was going to be blamed for the boys having to stay in the convent in Kilkenny, and then I thought about how the boys wouldn't love me any more either. I felt like I used to when I had to decide whether to take the tea chests to Mr Gleason, whom I hated, or whether to make the long journey to the farm. I thought hard.

'All right, Daddy. I'll try to like her.'

Daddy said I was a good girl and that it would be easier than I thought to get used to the new mammy.

'She won't go out and leave you alone to look after the boys,' he said. 'You'll all be taken care of. And listen to me, pet. It's important that the Minister knows we will all be happy together and that you're looking forward to going home. Do you understand?'

All I understood was that my real mammy was not coming back and that the new mammy was here to stay and that, for everyone's sake, I had to like her. I still didn't know who or what the Minister was but for some reason, we had to think about him too. I asked Daddy if the Minister was coming to live with us, and he laughed.

'Holy Mother of God, I hope not. We haven't got a chair big enough for his fat backside! Now, c'mon, let's go.'

We went out to the car and drove to the city centre. Daddy told me that we were going to see his legal team, and I asked him what sort of a game was legal.

He looked serious. 'These are the men who are fighting the government for me so that I can take you home again.'

We arrived in a busy, wide street near St Stephen's Green, and Daddy pulled up outside a tall house. He rang the bell on the front door and, while we waited for someone to answer, I stared at the shiny brass knocker. It was in the shape of a lady's face. She had a sad expression and there were grapes and feathers in her hair. I wanted to knock her against the door but Daddy stopped me.

A real lady opened the door. She wore a fancy skirt and blouse, and her hair was in a perfect bun at the back of her head. We followed her up a sweeping staircase to an office on the first landing. The carpet was so thick, our feet made no noise at all, and I wondered were we in some kind of palace. Daddy said there'd be a whole team here but when the door to the office opened, there was just one man. He was a giant, even bigger than the Reverend Mother. He had a shaggy, white beard and bushy eyebrows that met at the top of his nose, and his eyes were blue and kind. He bent down and shook my hand. His hands were huge and very clean, but not soft like the hands of the priests who said Mass at the convent. I could smell whiskey and pipe tobacco and soap.

'So you're the little minx that's giving everyone the trouble!' the giant man said, smiling at me.

'Evelyn, this is Mr Conolly,' Daddy said. 'He's helping us.'

Mr Conolly shook hands with Daddy and invited us both to sit down. I sat in one of the big leather chairs and slid right to the back so that my feet stuck out over the front edge of the chair. When I tried to pull myself back up so that I could sit properly, I discovered I was stuck. I would have to put my feet on the seat to get out again. I was afraid to do that and I didn't want to tell Daddy that I was stuck, so I just sat very still and listened to what Mr Conolly was saying.

'Desmond, why didn't you tell me that Mrs Brown wasn't a Catholic?'

Daddy took out a packet of Gold Flake and offered one to Mr Conolly. He lit his cigarette and inhaled deeply while he thought about the question.

After what seemed like ages, Daddy said, 'I don't know how they could find that out, it's not as if she goes to church. But so what if she's not a Catholic? What the shaggin hell has *that* to do with the price of bread?'

Oh no, Daddy was going to purgatory for sure now, cursing and mentioning a church in the same breath. I would be praying for the release of his soul until I was an old lady, and who was Mrs Brown, anyway?

Mr Conolly turned to look at me. He smiled very sweetly and started asking me questions about the nuns and the convent. I told him that the nuns were nice and that we went to school every day and that the food was fine, except for on Saturdays when we got black pudding, and I said that if you got ringworm, you had to have your head shaved and play by yourself in the coal yard.

'So I hope I never get ringworm,' I said.

I also told him that I got into trouble for not going to choir practice and that Mother Bernadette made me work on the farm.

'She gives it to me as penance because she doesn't know I love working on the farm.'

I looked over at Daddy. He was smiling at me.

'Don't tell on me,' I said to him, 'or I'll have to work in the boot room.'

'Don't worry, pet,' he said. 'I won't tell.'

'Now then, Evelyn,' Mr Conolly said. 'Tell me this. Do you like your new mammy?'

His question shocked me. I stared up at him from where I was, sunk way down in the leather chair. Was Mr Conolly the Minister? I looked at Daddy again. He was lighting another cigarette and his eyes met mine. I knew what he wanted me to say, but this big man was so kind and friendly that I wanted to tell him the truth: that I hated Jessie and that I wanted my real mammy back.

'Come on, little sweet,' Mr Conolly said. 'You can tell me.'

The things that Daddy had said to me that morning were all going through my mind. I would have to tell a lie now, for all our sakes, and I would make a confession before Mass on Sunday.

'Yes,' I said, 'I like her very much. She's pretty and she makes Daddy happy and I won't have to go to Mr Gleason's any more.'

I wasn't sure if that was enough. I hoped so because I couldn't think of any more nice things to say about the new mammy. Mr Conolly patted my head and went back to his desk. I managed to wriggle my way out of the big chair, and wandered around the room while Daddy and Mr Conolly talked some more. My ears pricked up when I heard the Minister mentioned.

'It's my guess,' Mr Conolly said, 'that the Minister is being got at. And I mean by our ecclesiastical friends. He is now trying to tell us that apart from not having your wife here to apply with you for Evelyn's release, the female assistance you have obtained is not acceptable.'

He picked up a letter and read part of it out to Daddy: 'Although your client has shown that he secured suitable accommodation and was in permanent employment, he has failed to obtain suitable female assistance in accordance with the Children Act, 1941.'

He handed the letter to Daddy, who scanned it and tossed it back on the desk in disgust. I could tell he was trying not to lose his temper.

'So what does this mean?' Daddy asked.

'What it means,' Mr Conolly said, 'is that they are going to use every dirty trick in the book. A friend of mine up at Leinster House owed me a favour. He tipped me off that a gentleman had made it his business to have a chat with Mrs Brown. And what this gentleman discovered was that Mrs Brown is not a Catholic. Therefore, Mrs Brown is not "suitable". What this means, Desmond, is that the clergy are taking an interest in your case.'

Daddy called someone a dirty bastard. His shoulders drooped and he let out a big sigh and pushed his hair back with his fingers. He looked tired.

'What do we do now?' he asked.

'We keep going,' Mr Conolly said. 'Ultimately, Mrs Brown's "suitability" is not the deciding factor.'

He handed me a lollipop and told me that if anyone asked me about the new mammy, I was to tell them exactly what I had told him.

'And for now,' he said, 'we'll leave it at that.'

He walked us out and down the stairs and, as I followed behind him and Daddy, I imagined sliding down the long, shiny wooden banister.

FIVE

As we left Mr Conolly's office and walked along St Stephen's Green towards the car, Daddy said he needed a drink. We got into the Austin and headed west, out of the city centre. He drove out along the Liffey and past the Phoenix Park. He didn't say where we were going, but I knew and was delighted. We were going to the Strawberry Beds, where Daddy'd lived as a boy. When we were all still together, before Mammy left, Daddy used to pile us into the Austin early on Sunday mornings, and we'd spend long sunny days on the river bank at the Strawberry Beds. The boys and I would collect sticks and dead branches, and Daddy would light a campfire. Mammy fried sausages and white pudding. Then she'd make a billycan of tea for Daddy. The rest of us just drank water, but it tasted special because we were drinking it by the river and having a lovely day out.

Then Daddy would find his minnow-fishing sack, where he'd stashed it in the bushes. He'd had the same one hidden in the same bush from the time he was sixteen. It was an old potato sack, and he'd slit one side of it and nailed two long brush handles along each of the cut edges. He would take his shoes and socks off and roll his trousers up to the knees and walk along the shallow side of the river, holding the sack out in front of him and scooping up the minnow for bait. Then he'd dump the bait in an old paint tin he'd washed out. I thought it was cruel to put the little squirming fish on a hook for a bigger fish to eat, but Daddy told me they couldn't feel anything.

'And when the salmon or the trout swallow them,' he said, 'it's instant death.'

One day, his sack was wriggling and jumping about as he lifted it from the water. We all gathered round to see what was giving the sack this life of its own. Daddy upended the sack over the paint tin and a huge eel slithered out and knocked the tin over in the grass. The eel slipped back into the river, and we all ran screaming to Mammy, shouting that Daddy had caught a snake.

'It's not a snake at all,' Daddy said, laughing. 'It's a kind of a fish.'

But we weren't convinced and it was a long time before any of us would paddle around in the river again.

If Daddy caught a fat trout or a salmon, Mammy would put the old black frying pan on the fire. The poor fish would get sizzled to a golden brown and we'd put slices of it between bread with tomato and onion. Afterwards, we'd have apple pie that Mammy had made the day before. Every time we had the fresh fish, Daddy would smack his lips and say, 'That's the best dinner I've ever had.'

Then he would lie back on the grass and smoke a cigarette while Mammy and I cleared up the campsite and washed the pan and the dishes in the river. After that, Daddy would take us to the Wren's Nest. He and Mammy would get a drink and sit inside the pub while the boys and I took our bags of crisps and bottles of lemonade and went outside.

Mammy always said, 'Mind the babies, or else!'

But we were always content on the days we went to the Strawberry Beds, and we'd sit happily on the grass, not causing any trouble, waiting for Mammy and Daddy to finish their drinks. Sometimes, we went back to the river afterwards and ran wild for the rest of the afternoon while Daddy fished some more.

One morning at the Strawberry Beds, I got into trouble. As we picked our way along the trodden track to the river bank, Daddy told me to hold John's hand because John was only a little fellow.

'And don't let him run away,' he said.

But John wriggled free and fell straight into a clump of nettles. He let out an ear-splitting scream and Daddy got stung himself pulling John out. Mammy slapped my legs for letting John fall and I started screaming too. Daddy was in bad humour then, but when Mammy started cooking the sausages, he came back to his old self. He wrapped John in dock leaves from head to toe and took his photograph. I was in the photo too, alongside John and still sulking because Mammy had slapped me. I loved the days at the Strawberry Beds, even that one, and sometimes I thought of them when I was feeling lonely for my brothers and for Mammy.

Now Daddy and I were back at the Wren's Nest. He parked the car on the grass, and we went inside. My eyes had to adjust to the gloom. A few old men were sitting chatting and smoking pipes. They all had pint glasses of porter in front of them on the bar. One or two looked up to see who had come in and nodded at Daddy. A squat, fat woman came through a door behind the bar, and Daddy ordered a pint of beer.

'Dessie Doyle! Is that you?' the woman asked, looking at him with surprise and smiled.

Daddy said, 'It's me.' But then he admitted that he couldn't place the woman.

It turned out that Daddy and the woman had been at school together, and they spent a few minutes catching up on old times. They laughed about this and that, and some of the men at the bar joined in. It seemed as though everyone in the pub remembered Daddy from when he'd been a young boy.

'I can remember your poor mammy and your lovely sister,' one of the old men said. He shook his head sadly and added that it was God's will that they had died so young.

Daddy told him that his other sister Annie had died of TB, and the old man blessed himself and took a sip of his porter.

I couldn't imagine Daddy as a boy. He seemed more relaxed now than he had in Mr Conolly's office. His drink was nearly gone, and the lady behind the bar invited him to stay for some tea, but he told her he had to be getting me back to the convent. Everybody knew what that meant.

'Have you had a bit of trouble, Des?' the woman asked him.

Daddy told her that Mammy had left the family and that now the 'bastard government' wouldn't let him have his children back.

I finished my lemonade and Daddy said goodbye to the old men. They all wished him good luck and the fat woman said she would pray for him.

On the way back to the convent, Daddy grew quiet again. When he hugged me goodbye at the convent door,

I could feel the old lump in my chest. I had heard a lot that day that I didn't understand, but I knew that the government was powerful and that Daddy was fighting them.

That night, I had a nightmare. I was on the banks of the river at the Strawberry Beds, and Daddy was lying under the water with a very sad look on his face. Mammy was standing on the bank in her bare feet, and I couldn't get past her to help Daddy out of the river.

One morning, as we were coming out of the orchard gate to go to school, I heard a man with a camera asking Mother Bridget if she would point me out to him. Mother Bridget told him to clear off and said that if he took a photograph of me without the Reverend Mother's permission, he would be in real trouble. After the man had gone, I asked Mother Bridget why the man would want a photograph of me.

She called my friend Siobhán over and said, 'Run ahead now to school with Evelyn and don't talk to anyone or stop for anything.'

Siobhán and I ran as fast as we could all the way to Lark Hill and were both out of breath by the time we reached the playground. When the rest of the girls arrived, they crowded round me and asked what was going on, but I couldn't answer. But it didn't seem too important.

The next morning, Mother Bernadette told me to come to see her before I went to school and to bring Siobhán with me. She looked very serious, and I wondered if she'd found out about the gang of us that had sneaked into the nuns' dormitory.

We hadn't touched anything, we'd just had a little look.

Not that there was much to see; all the beds were hidden inside curtained cubicles. We'd dashed past the cubicles, trying not to make too much noise with our boots on the polished floor. We flew out the door and hurried towards the back stairs and slid all the way down the curving banister. One of the women who worked in the laundry saw us at the bottom of the stairs.

'What are you young rips doing here?' she said. She was trying to sound mad.

We said nothing, just ran like scared rabbits to the coal yard and hid there, bent double at the waist and trying to catch our breath and laughing at the same time. When we calmed down, we discussed the question of whether or not we would go to confession. I said that I wasn't going to confess, and the others said they wouldn't either, and we all agreed that it would be our secret.

So I didn't think it was the trip to the dormitory that Mother Bernadette wanted to see me about. Maybe she'd found out about Mary Kelly and me in the boot room. We'd sneaked in and mixed up all the boots and tied the laces together, causing uproar. No one could find their right size, and some of the knots we'd tied were so tight they couldn't be undone. Mother Paul had to cut them with scissors. She rushed around looking for new laces, trying to make sure none of us was late for school. I wanted to own up about the boot room, but Mary convinced me to keep my mouth shut, and we all got the strap as a result.

As I sat there over my breakfast, wondering what kind of trouble I was in with Mother Bernadette, I got so worried, I couldn't eat. I just wanted to get the whole thing over with, whatever it was. Finally, Siobhán and I left the refectory and headed towards Mother Bernadette's office. We held hands on the way. The office was at the very end of the corridor, and it was more like a big cupboard than a proper office. I was shaking with fright, and Siobhán was trying to reassure me that everything was all right and that surely I was not in trouble with Mother Bernadette. Siobhán was like the big sister I never had. I loved her shiny black hair and her clear pale skin and her beautiful singing, except when she'd sung 'Oh My Papa' for the hundredth time in one day. 'Can you sing "Far Away" instead?' I'd asked once and she threatened to box my ears.

Outside Mother Bernadette's office she straightened my tie and tightened my ribbons. In her best imitation of the Reverend Mother, she said: 'Courage child.'

I giggled, and Mother Bernadette opened the door. She didn't look angry, and I knew straight away that I wasn't in trouble.

'Come in, girls,' she said. 'Sit down.'

She began by telling Siobhán that it was very important that she listen carefully to everything she was about to say.

'You are one of the older girls,' she said, 'and we are going to rely on you to take extra special care of Evelyn.'

Siobhán's eyes were wide and she nodded solemnly.

Mother Bernadette turned her attention to me. 'Evelyn, your Daddy is going to court today to ask the Minister if you can go home, and we are expecting that the newspapers will be very interested in the case.'

I was going home! I could hardly sit still. My heart was thumping and my hands were shaking.

'We anticipate, however, that the court hearings will take some time. Yesterday, a newspaper photographer tried to take your picture. Now, we don't want that to happen. Do you understand, Evelyn?'

I said that I understood. I didn't want my picture in the papers either, and I couldn't understand why anyone would want to put it there. It was Daddy who was fighting with the Minister, not me.

'Siobhán,' Mother Bernadette said, 'I want you to make sure that Evelyn is with you at all times. When you are in the street on your way to school, keep her on the inside of the path and, if you see anyone with a big camera, you are to pull Evelyn's hood up and make your way to school as quickly as possible. Either that, or you bring her straight back here. Can you do that, dear?'

Siobhán nodded again and managed to look even more solemn than she had a minute ago.

Over the next few days, she stuck close to me and glared at all the men we saw on the street, even though none of them had cameras. Siobhán took her duties very seriously, and we both found it exciting. Every journey to and from Lark Hill became an adventure, as we pointed at the men and said, 'He might be one,' or 'What about him?' I would pull up my hood and walk like a monk in prayer, my head bowed, my hands clasped together and hidden by my sleeves. Sometimes, the other girls would join in and pretend to be monks as well, and we'd all chant gibberish and moan long, loud 'Amens'. We got some queer looks from the grown-ups on the street, but it was great craic, and I was sure that with Siobhán guarding me, there was no chance that my photograph would get into the papers.

*

It was May, and Daddy was in the High Court, straining to hear what was being said. Mr Conolly was explaining to the three judges that when Daddy had consented to have his children committed to the State industrial schools, the justice in the Children's Court had advised him 'not to leave the children there too long'. Naturally, Mr Conolly pointed out, Daddy had left the Children's Court with the impression that he could retrieve his children from the schools when he was ready.

'As Mr Doyle had no legal counsel at the time, he had no reason to think otherwise. Surely Your Honours can imagine how alarmed Mr Doyle must have been when he was told that he could do no such thing. And, that the reason his daughter would not be released into his custody was, and I quote from the Minister's letter to Mr Doyle, "that it would not be in the best interests of the child". We have here,' he said, motioning towards Daddy, 'a father who has a home and the means to support his child. And yet that child is being maintained at the expense of the taxpayer.'

He paused for effect, then picked up a piece of paper off his desk and waved it in the air. It was another one of the Minister's letters to Daddy.

'Mr Doyle has fulfilled the conditions set out in this communication from the Minister. Now, however, the Minister's learned counsel has discovered that the application submitted by my client for the return of his child is invalid. The Minster's counsel now demands that Mr Doyle locate his wife and persuade her to sign their children over to him.'

This mention of Mammy and her signature led once again to the argument over the word 'parents' in the Children Act, and how, exactly, the legislators had intended that word to be interpreted. The judges and the Minister's counsel were insisting that 'parents' meant Mammy and Daddy together; Mr Conolly claimed otherwise. The argument had gone on for over an hour, and it was becoming obvious to Daddy that Mr Conolly was losing.

Daddy got up and left the courtroom. He needed some air or a drink. He walked along Ormond Quay, over the Ha'penny Bridge and found a pub on Temple Bar. With a shot of whiskey and a pint of porter in front of him, he sat in the snug mulling over his plans to 'kidnap' his children, trying to imagine how it could work and what the consequences might be. The first time he'd discussed it with Granddad, Granddad had suggested taking me to Belfast himself. But Daddy had since decided that *he* should take me and have Granddad follow with the boys. The two of us would catch the ferry from Belfast to Stranraer, in Scotland, and head to England from there. Daddy wondered if he'd have to change our surname once we got across the water. What if the police arrested us in England? Would they send me back to Ireland for the Minister to decide what would become of me? And what if Granddad wasn't able to take the boys out of the convent? He hated the thought of them being trapped in Ireland, unable to join us in England, if we did get that far. Daddy made up his mind. He would organise an outing for one day soon, take all of us out together and not bring us back. We would have at least six hours' head start, and we could be on the ferry before the nuns missed us. He felt a sense of resolution, and he finished his drink and headed back to the Four Courts.

When Daddy took his seat at the barristers' table, Mr Beatty turned to look at him. He was surprised to see Daddy so calm and relaxed, and he hoped that he hadn't had too many drinks. He needn't have worried. Daddy was sober and he'd no intention of making a scene. He had his own plan now and, even if it meant living among the 'cursed English', at least he would have his children back, and that was all that mattered to him. He turned his attention to Mr Conolly, who was speaking.

'Your Honours,' he said, 'I quote Ulysses S. Grant, 18th President of the United States, who said, in his Inaugural Address, "I know of no method to secure the repeal of bad or obnoxious laws so effective as their stringent execution."'

Daddy didn't understand how all the justices and barristers could be so polite to each other when they were on opposing sides. And what was all this 'poetry and Latin stuff?' Mr Beatty whispered to him that Mr Conolly was fond of quoting philosophers and statesmen.

'He can make his feelings known without risking being in contempt of court. And sometimes,' he added, 'he uses other people's words as veiled threats of his own intentions.'

'I draw your attention to Article 42 of the Irish Constitution,' Mr Conolly continued, 'which upholds the right of a parent to direct the education of his child. With all due respect, Your Honours, I submit that the detention of Evelyn Doyle, and the section of the Children Act enabling that detention, are repugnant to the Constitution.

'I respectfully request the Court for an order of *habeas corpus* directing the Minister for Education and the Manager of the school to bring the child before the court to be given to her father on the grounds that her continued detention is contrary to the provisions of the Constitution.'

He sat down, and Justice McLoughlin spoke.

'It is a tragic case,' he said, 'and no adjective I can think of can adequately express the degree of reluctance with which I conclude that the child must remain in the custody of the State. However, it is the duty of this Court to administer the law as it finds it and not as it would like to find it.'

The judge then acknowledged that Mr Conolly had raised a matter relating to constitutionality, and he reminded him that the High Court did not have jurisdiction over constitutional matters.

Mr Conolly got to his feet, greatly encouraged by the obvious show of sympathy from the bench. He requested leave to appeal to the Supreme Court, and his request was granted. The judges upheld his contention that Section 10 of the Children Act was invalid and referred the question of its validity to the Supreme Court. Mr Conolly looked pleased, but to Daddy it was just another court. After all he had his plan.

When Daddy and his counsel stepped outside the Four Courts, they were greeted by the dazzling flash of cameras. A man rushed up to Daddy and asked him how he felt about the day's result. Mr Beatty wedged himself between the reporter and Daddy and explained that they were disappointed they hadn't got a decision in their favour from the High Court that day, but they would continue their fight in the Supreme Court. Behind them, Mr Conolly was giving an interview to another reporter.

After the press drifted away, Mr Conolly explained to Daddy that he granted the interview because they were going to need all the public support they could get.

'The people need to understand what's happening, Desmond. And once they do, they'll be on your side. How could the ordinary citizen not be moved by the plight of a father fighting for the right to bring his children home? Take heart, my boy!'

With that, he waved a cheery farewell and told Daddy that he would be in touch sooner rather than later.

Daddy asked Mr Beatty and Nick to join him for a drink.

'I have something to tell you,' he said.

They went to a pub and settled into a quiet corner, and Daddy described to them his plans to take my brothers and me out of the country. He said he felt it was only fair to tell them, so that they wouldn't waste any more of their time preparing for further court hearings.

'Who's going to pay all you people if this goes on and on?' he asked. 'It frightens me to think that if we lose any more hearings, I'll be working to pay off your bills for the rest of my life. I've made my decision,' he said. 'I'm taking my children and getting the feck out of this country.'

Nick said he wasn't going to listen to any more of this nonsense and he got up to leave.

'Talk some sense into him, why don't you?' he told Mr Beatty.

Mr Beatty tried to convince Daddy of how foolish his plan was.

'For one thing, there is no way you are going to be allowed to take all the children out on the same day. Some eejit already tried that, and he might've got away with it, too, if he hadn't taken them straight home to the farm in Mayo. And, even if you did manage to get them all out together, you'd surely get caught down the line.'

He reminded Daddy of the judges' sympathy in court that day and said now that they were on their way to the Supreme Court, it was not the time to be doing anything rash or illegal.

'TJ is going through the Constitution with a fine-toothed comb,' he said. 'He's focusing on your right to direct Evelyn's education. It's right there in Article 42, Desmond, and it could be exactly what we need to challenge this law they're using to keep the children from you. So please,' he said, 'just be patient. I'll keep you fully informed of whatever progress we make.'

Mr Beatty and Daddy shook hands, but Daddy didn't promise anything.

Daddy stayed a while longer in the pub, not feeling up to facing Granddad or Jessie just yet. They had all been convinced that Mr Conolly would win today and had even planned a quiet celebration for that evening.

Someone in the pub turned on the wireless, and David Whitfield was crooning the latest hit, 'Answer Me, Oh My Lord'. Daddy snorted with derision, swallowed the dregs of his beer and left. He walked back over the Ha'Penny Bridge and saw a long funeral cortège crawling up the quays. At its head was a glass-sided hearse, pulled by four magnificent jet-black horses. People on the street stopped to bless themselves, and Daddy asked an old man who it was that had died.

'The saintly Dr Kathleen Lynn,' the old man said.

Kathleen Lynn had opened the first children's hospital in Dublin, at the turn of the century.

'Oh, she was a saint all right,' the old man went on. 'She took care of my five little ones till they died of TB.'

He dabbed at his rheumy eyes and lost interest in Daddy.

When Daddy was a boy, he'd had so many friends die of TB that, after a while, it was hardly a shock anymore. His best friend Gussie Hair-oil had lost twelve brothers and sisters to TB, and now Gussie Hair-oil was the only one left of his whole brood.

Watching the cortège pass, Daddy thought about how we were all still alive. He knew he should be grateful for that.

Ginny was one of my friends from school who lived with her family at home. The morning after Daddy's last day in the High Court, she grabbed me as I walked into the cloak-room.

'Quick, Evelyn, come into the lav. I have something to show you.'

I followed her to a toilet cubicle, and she pulled a news-paper from her school bag. There, on the front page, was a picture of me, coming out of the school gate. Over the photograph was a huge headline: FATHER CANNOT GET CUSTODY OF DAUGHTER.

I ran to look for Siobhán. I was mortified; I thought

everyone I passed in the halls must know that Daddy had lost. I ran into Miss O'Donnell, our teacher, and she found Siobhán for me and told her to take me back to the convent. We ran most of the way. All I could see was the path because I had the hood of my cloak pulled well down over my face. Siobhán kept a tight hold of my hand so I wouldn't trip. We slipped inside the green gates to the orchard and pushed them shut behind us and leaned against them to catch our breath.

Now that I had a minute to think, the meaning of the headline struck me. I broke down and cried and banged the gate door with my fists. I was never going to get out of here. Siobhán tried to comfort me and led me by the hand to Mother Bernadette's office. Mother Bernadette was surprised to see us, but she realised immediately that something had happened to upset us. She rushed over to me and started to help me off with my cloak and boots.

'What is it, child?' she asked Siobhán.

Poor Siobhán felt responsible. She was trying not to cry but tears were filling her eyes.

'I'm sorry, Mother,' she said, 'I swear I didn't see anyone with a camera. But Evelyn's picture is in the paper, and it says that her daddy lost and can't bring her home now.'

She blew her nose quietly and snuffled a bit, then blessed herself. Mother Bernadette took us both into the sewing room. She lit the fire, which had been set for the evening, and left the room. When she came back a few minutes later, the fire was blazing. I sat there staring into the flames, trying not to think about anything, but the big fire and the awful feeling I had reminded me of the night Daddy'd burned all the photographs of Mammy. Siobhán was sitting on the armrest of my chair, saying over and over again how sorry she was. She had her arm around me. Mother Bernadette told her that it wasn't her fault and that even if she had seen the photographer, there was nothing she could have done.

'You're not to worry,' she said. 'The bowsie was probably disguised as a lamp post or something.'

She smiled kindly and told us to dry our tears, and then she said a short prayer. Mother Imelda came in, carrying a tray with tea and cream cakes. Siobhán and I drank our tea from the nuns' delicate china cups, and it made me think of Granny's lovely kitchen.

We didn't have to go back to school that day and by the time night came, I felt a little calmer. But I woke in the middle of the night after a bad dream, and I was hot all over and my throat hurt. I cried out for Mother Paul, who was on night duty. Before she came in, I made sure that my arms were folded across my chest and that I was lying rigidly on my back.

Mother Paul held a little lamp over me and said, 'Child! You look like you have the mumps.'

She helped me out of bed and took me to the infirmary and handed me over to Sister Francis, who she said would look after me.

Sister Frances was dressed in black, not like the nuns I normally saw, whose habits were all white. She was an old lady and very gentle. She smiled a lot and called me 'Evey dear' and said that I was to call her Sister. I couldn't be bothered calling her anything for the first few days; I looked as though I had two giant gobstoppers in my mouth. As I began to get better, a lot of the other girls started to get sick. One by one, they appeared in the infirmary, all with the same enormous lumps on one or both sides of their faces. I couldn't help thinking how funny they looked.

Sister Frances insisted that we all eat a blood orange every day. I hated them and tried to give mine away, but she would stand beside my bed until I had eaten every last section. If she'd thought it would do us good, she'd have persuaded us to eat the skin as well. She made French toast for us as a special treat and just generally spoiled us and made us feel loved. It was a new experience for me, being looked after like this, and it more than made up for the lumps and the sore throat. But every night, before we went to sleep, we had to drink a spoonful of bitter thick medicine. This dreadful black stuff guaranteed that none of us would try to linger in the infirmary once we felt better.

Daddy and Granddad visited me at the infirmary one day. I saw them before they saw me, and Daddy's face looked so pale and worried that I wanted to cry. But when he caught sight of me bouncing on the bed and calling him, his face broke into a wide smile. He rushed over to me and scooped me up in his arms and twirled me round and round until I squealed with joy. Granddad had brought me some sweets and a bag of oranges. I didn't have the heart to tell him that I couldn't eat another orange if my life depended on it. I kept quiet and gave them to the other girls after Daddy and Granddad had gone. Daddy'd seen the photograph in the paper, and Mother Bernadette had told him how upset I'd been. He wanted to know if I was all right.

'Yes,' I said, 'but I want to go home.'

Because of my mumps, Daddy'd had to put off his plan of taking me to Scotland. In the meantime, Mr Beatty had persuaded him to drop the idea altogether and wait for the court's decision. Daddy tried to be optimistic. He was still hoping that the Corporation was going to give him a house so that he would have a place for us if we all came home. When the boys turned eleven, they would be sent from the convent to the Christian Brothers, and time was running out for Noel and Maurice. Daddy didn't like the Christian Brothers. He called them the Bastard Brothers because it was rumoured that they beat Christianity into the boys they were supposed to be teaching.

Granny still sent me the ¼lb packets of tea and the green ribbons every month. I looked forward to her parcels, and I loved her for not forgetting me. I was still managing to keep Granny's packages a secret from Daddy, but I felt a bit guilty about it and confessed to the priest every Saturday. I had the same sins each week: not saying my prayers, being disobedient, having uncharitable thoughts – whatever they were – and not telling Daddy about my secret with Granny.

In early summer, towards the end of that year's final school term, I was leaving for school through the orchard gate when I was met by four or five men. A couple of them were shouting questions at me, and the others had gigantic cameras. The flashbulbs blinded me; for a second, I stood there, petrified and confused. Siobhán had been relieved of her duties as my guard by then, so I was all alone that morning. I turned around and ran back through the gate, slamming it behind me. I saw Mother Bernadette and Mother Bridget and told them what had happened, and they hurried to the gate and sent the men away. For the rest of the term, I wasn't allowed to go to school with the other girls, and the nuns gave me my lessons alone at the convent.

With the coming of another summer, I felt I'd been in the convent for a very long time. There were whole days now when I didn't think about my brothers. I hadn't forgotten them, I just didn't worry about them like I used to or wonder what they were doing all the time. Daddy brought me the news about them, and I gave him my books and comics to pass on to the boys whenever he was going to Kilkenny.

The summer months were warm, and I was happy at the convent. We spent the long, sunny days in the fields and helped out on the farm. I liked the six pigs and gave names to each one, but the cows frightened me, and I avoided the farmyard when they were being herded to the milking shed. Mother Teresa and some of the older girls had helped me to make new clothes for my doll Molly, and now Molly had a beautiful green cloak of her own to go with her white dolly shoes. She was loved by all the girls and went everywhere with us. By the time that summer had ended, Molly'd lost her voice and was looking the worse for wear.

Little Ann McCafferty got ringworm. The nuns shaved her hair off, and she had to play alone in the coal yard. One day, when I was coming down the stairs from the dormitory, I spotted Ann from the landing window. She was playing by herself in the yard, and she looked so lonely. I watched for a minute or two. I wanted to wave to her, and I knocked on the window to get her attention. But she didn't look up; the noise from the laundry boilers was too loud and she couldn't hear me. I went back up to the dormitory and took Molly from her cupboard and sneaked past the boot room and out of the back door. I gave Molly to Ann to keep her company and it seemed to cheer Ann up a little. Mother Imelda nearly had a fit when she found out I'd been with Ann, and she made me strip off and get into a bath that smelled like a hospital.

As she scrubbed my head with an evil-smelling soap, she said, 'What would your father say if he came and found his daughter with ringworm and no hair?'

When I got Molly back, all her new clothes had disappeared, and she was blacker than the coal in the yard. It put me in a terrible temper. The girls in my dormitory helped me to give her a bath and, as I watched them holding Molly down head first under the water, I hoped that if any of them ever had a real baby, they wouldn't bathe it like that. Siobhán said that she would help Mother Teresa make a brand new outfit for Molly, and she promised that she would even sew her another green cloak.

Friday nights, we all lined up outside the bathroom, and the nuns would cut our hair and nails. I was the only girl who didn't have to get her hair cut. Whichever nun was on cutting duty would just trim the ends. No matter how much I begged them to make my hair look just like the other girls', they wouldn't hear of it. Daddy had forbidden them to cut it, and that was that.

'And what would you do with all those lovely green ribbons your granny sends you?' Mother Imelda would say.

One night, before we went to bed, some of the bigger girls wound strands of my hair in thin strips of rags. The next morning, when they took the rags out, I had a lovely mass of ringlets, just like a little American girl I had seen in a picture somewhere. Later that morning, the Reverend Mother met me in the corridor and stopped dead in her tracks. She took me to Mother Imelda and instructed her to do away with my ringlets. In no time, Mother Imelda had my head under the tap. She told me that fixing my hair like that was vain and a sin, and she tut-tutted a lot as she soaked my hair till every curl had vanished. But I could tell by her voice that she wasn't annoyed with me.

On rainy days, Mother Teresa helped us to make socks with four needles. Her patience was infinite, especially with the girls like me who had never seen a knitting needle before, let alone used one. I was very proud the day I finally managed to finish my first sock. Because it had taken me the entire summer to complete, it was also my last sock, but having only half a pair didn't lessen my sense of accomplishment in the least.

We took more day trips to the seaside with the Lord Mayor. One of the days was cold and windy, but we waded out into the sea anyway, our dresses tucked into our knickers. We got sand in our sandwiches and there were goose bumps on our legs, but we had a great time. I felt totally carefree, not having babies to mind or my small brothers to look after, and I ran wild with the other girls. It was a golden summer. My favourite days were the ones when the threshers came to make winter hay. We played and rolled around the hay barn. The nuns brought us our dinner in the field and we ate with the smell of new-mown grass all around us.

The Supreme Court would hear Daddy's case in October. As the date drew nearer, the press became more and more attentive. Stories appeared in the papers regularly. When the new school term started, the nuns decided not to put me back into Lark Hill until the case was settled. I was jealous watching the girls go off in the mornings with their new emerald-green winter cloaks, and I missed seeing my friends from school who didn't live at the convent. But the nuns spoiled me and gave me many treats that the other girls didn't get.

At first, I didn't realise that the papers were still interested in me, but the girls at school who lived at home heard about it from their parents and gave the convent girls the news. A few of them even smuggled press cuttings to my friends, and the older girls at the convent started a scrapbook, which they kept hidden from the nuns. Some started talking about 'when Evelyn goes home', knowing full well that if Daddy won his case and beat the government, some of them would get to go home too. I still prayed for Siobhán and hoped that her daddy would come for her soon. Now, I thought, my daddy *had* to win his case because so many of the girls in the convent were depending on him.

A few times when Daddy came to visit, he brought Jessie with him. Gradually, I was starting to accept that my real mammy was never coming back and that Jessie was here to stay.

One day, the three of us went to Avoca, a lovely village in Wicklow, and Daddy brought his fishing rod with him. I didn't have my brothers to play with, and Jessie and I grew bored watching Daddy fish, so we wandered round the village. She took me to a café, and we ordered tea and scones. She told me that the two of us should try to 'get on', for Daddy's sake, and she said that when the boys and I were allowed to come home again, we could all have a happy time together. I told her that I missed my own mammy, and I asked her if she thought Mammy would ever come home.

'No, love. I shouldn't think so.' And then she said very quietly, as though speaking to herself, 'There's never a way back.'

Her eyes had a faraway look that made me think she was going to cry. But she didn't. She just took a deep breath and lit another cigarette and ordered more tea. After a while, we went back to the spot that Daddy was fishing. It was a little pool in the river, surrounded by large trees. Jessie decided that she would have a go at fishing, and she tied a piece of string to a long stick and hooked a safety pin to the end of the string. I watched in horror as she put her hand into Daddy's bait tin and pulled out a big worm and stuck it on the pin. How could a lady do that? She dangled the line over the water.

Almost immediately, she shouted, 'Dessie, quick! What'll I do? I've got one!'

The stick was jerking wildly, and she managed to lift it a bit out of the water. Hooked on the pin was a good-sized trout. Daddy took the trout off the hook and said that the poor fish had either committed suicide or been a victim of beginner's luck. But Jessie insisted her natural talent had landed the trout.

'You either have it or you don't,' she said, and turned her nose in the air and gave Daddy a snooty look, very pleased with herself.

I laughed at the banter between them and thought that maybe everything was going to be fine after all with this new mammy. I hadn't seen Daddy and my real mammy laughing together like this, and I decided that I would try to 'get on' with Jessie. After that, it started to get easier, calling her Mammy.

Jessie told me many stories about England, and I passed them on to the girls in my dormitory. After each of my visits with Daddy and Jessie, the girls would be waiting eagerly for the next instalment. I embellished the stories to make them more interesting and implied, though I didn't actually say, that my new mammy knew the Queen of England. I was enjoying all the attention that came with having an English mammy. When Jessie gave me the latest invention, called a 'Biro', I was in great demand. It was only a ballpoint pen, but suddenly, all the girls had something they needed urgently to write and were forever asking me for the loan of my Biro. The nuns wouldn't let me use it for schoolwork. Mother Paul said it was only a fad and would never catch on. She told us we were better off learning how to write properly with pen and ink. I was sure she was wrong. When I used the pen and ink, I always got stains between my first two fingers and blots in my copy books, but with the Biro, there was never a mess.

When the Biro went dry I was sure I'd broken it, and I was frightened to tell Jessie. But she figured it out herself, though, because she soon bought me a refill and explained to me how it worked. After that, I included Jessie in my nightly prayers. I didn't leave my real mammy out, I just put her at the end. I still didn't like it when Daddy held Jessie's hand or put his arm around her shoulder. He hadn't done those things with my real mammy and, though I didn't know why, I found it unsettling.

When Daddy came to visit, in the weeks leading up to the Supreme Court hearings, he would often have two or three men from the newspapers with him. It was part of Mr Conolly's plan to drum up public support. I felt shy and didn't say much and wished the men would go away. They were always asking me questions about the nuns and about what life was like in the convent. They even wanted to know what we ate for breakfast and tea. I made up stories about having the best butter for our bread and steak for dinner and jelly and custard every single day. I told them that we never got black pudding and that sometimes we were so full, we couldn't get up from the table. This made them all laugh, even Daddy. But Daddy got annoyed when one of the men asked me how I liked my new English mammy.

'Mrs Brown is my housekeeper, if you don't mind,' Daddy said, 'so don't be asking the child those kind of questions.'

Sometimes a man with a camera would come with Daddy and tell us to stand here, there and everywhere. I never smiled in the photographs. I didn't like how the man was taking up my precious time with Daddy.

Daddy said, 'Try to be nice to these men, pet. They're going to help you get out of the convent.' He never explained how they would help.

At the time, Granddad couldn't come to visit as often. He was getting ready to play his cello in the Gaiety Theatre's orchestra for the Festival of Italian Opera. He hadn't played in the orchestra for a couple of years and was looking forward to seeing his old friends again.

'Wear something decent,' Daddy warned him.

Granddad was careless about some things and would often put on an old jersey with holes in the elbows and an ancient tweed jacket that Daddy said he'd been wearing forever. But his shoes were always polished, and he still wore stiff white collars that he fastened onto his shirt with brass studs. Daddy said Granddad should have changed the shirt as often as he changed the collar. Granddad huffed and puffed and called Daddy 'the big I am' and continued dressing in his usual way, quoting one of his favourite sayings. 'The fact that boys are allowed to exist at all is evidence of a remarkable Christian forbearance among men.'

'I'm only trying to be helpful,' Daddy said.

One night, during rehearsals, Granddad nearly got his marching orders. The guest conductor, a hot-tempered Italian called Morelli, had seen Granddad tying a knot in one of the strings of his cello after it snapped. Morelli had watched, with morbid fascination, as Granddad played a solo. Afterwards, he told Granddad that his nerves had been stretched tighter than the string and said he wouldn't be able to bear the strain if he had to go through all that again, on a night when paying customers were there. He instructed Granddad to replace the string at once.

Granddad became indignant. In a quiet and dignified

manner, he explained that he knew more about his cello strings than Morelli, 'the foreign eejit', knew about spaghetti. In the thirty years he'd played, Granddad had tied his strings more than once. The other members of the orchestra sometimes ran a book on the odds of one of Granddad's strings snapping in the middle of a solo, but he'd never had a mishap during a performance. He had even played 'The Dying Swan' solo from *Swan Lake* with a knot in one of his strings.

Daddy tried to arrange to take my brothers and me to see the new Walt Disney picture *The Lady and the Tramp*, but he was not allowed to take us all out at once; Mr Beatty had been right. So he took Jessie and me on our own. Now that the hearings were so close, though, Daddy had to be careful about being seen with Jessie in public. She was supposed to be his housekeeper, and he was a bit nervous about attracting any negative publicity. Jessie played along with the game. She knew well that this was a Catholic country and that a man living with an English Protestant as though she were his wife was a situation likely to cause problems. I played the game too. I had reluctantly accepted Jessie as my mammy but I had to make sure not to let on that she was anything more than Daddy's housekeeper. Daddy told me not to talk to anyone about my new mammy, especially not to the men from the newspaper who came with him when he visited me at the convent.

With the press following the story and editorials appearing more often in the papers, Daddy had been receiving letters of support from all over the country. People told him they were praying for him. They wished him luck and urged him to carry on with his fight. It worried him because he felt that he was being seen as some kind of hero. He just wanted to get his children back, but now he was being swept up in all this attention that he didn't want and couldn't very well cope with. All over Dublin, people recognized him. Perfect strangers would come up to him and shake his hand and wish him well. Women were forever blessing themselves when they met him and telling him they'd be praying for him. It seemed the whole of Ireland was praying for Daddy, and he worried that if he lost, he would be the object of so much pity he wouldn't be able to bear it.

His local pub set up an appeal fund to help with the legal costs, and everyone contributed generously. Soon the pennies, threepenny bits and sixpences added up to a fair amount. When the case was mentioned on the wireless, a hush would fall over the pub and, afterwards, a robust discussion would follow and everyone would give his or her opinion on the matter. Mostly, Daddy stayed out of the arguments. He would just listen and whisper to Granddad that everybody was suddenly an expert on children and the law.

The Supreme Court hearings were set to begin on October 12th, and Daddy's legal team had three more weeks to prepare their case. They were going to build on the arguments that Mr Conolly had introduced at the close of their appearance in the High Court. Mr Conolly would argue that Daddy should be able, without Mammy's consent, to take me out of the convent, and he would claim that the section of the Children Act that prevented him from doing so contravened Article 42 of the Constitution, which gave Daddy the right to direct my education, and Article 41, which gave a parent and child the fundamental mutual right to each other's society.

Around that time, the Corporation sent Daddy and his team down to the country on a painting job, and I didn't see him for over a week. Since the time he'd come back from England, I had seen him every few days and now that I wasn't able to, I felt unsettled. Jessie found his absence particularly difficult because she never knew if there would be a reporter on the doorstep when she went out, and Daddy had instructed her not to talk to anybody, in case she slipped up.

'They can be devious bastards,' he warned her.

Jessie hadn't bargained for any of this, and there were times she thought about boarding a ferry and going back to England. She still found Granddad difficult to deal with, and especially now, with Daddy away. He wouldn't let her cook or clean for him, and she realised it was easier to make do with a sandwich in the evening than to attempt a meal. She drank lots of tea and smoked thirty or forty cigarettes a day. By the time Daddy came home from the country, Jessie was like a skeleton. He scolded her for not looking after herself. He didn't realise how hard it was for her, being cooped up in a house with a cantankerous old man, frightened even to go to the local shops for the messages.

What Daddy also didn't know was that he had come home just in time to stop Jessie going back to England.

Ever since she could remember, she'd rushed into things.

She had married David to get out of her mother's house and the unbearable situation there. After Jessie's father had died in World War I, when Jessie was still a child, her mother had married a cruel and selfish man. Jessie had gone to work in the family chip shop at the age of eleven. Her schooling had suffered, and she'd carried the stink of grease in her clothes. The other kids in her class avoided sitting beside her and she felt lonely and ashamed.

When she'd met David, he'd seemed like the answer to her problems. In the beginning, the marriage was all right, but as David's drinking grew worse, Jessie had to struggle harder and harder to make ends meet. She'd been forced to take in lodgers and had got odd menial jobs in factory canteens to supplement her income. David decided that he didn't have to work at all. Then, during World War II, he was called up. Jessie went to work in a munitions factory. The war years, strangely, had been the best and happiest of her life. But when the war had ended, her miserable existence with David had resumed.

When she'd met Daddy, she saw another chance at happiness. She'd never expected that she would wind up in a situation that might cause her even more heartache and grief than life with David had.

She didn't want to leave him, but she was sure that if she didn't get out of that house soon, she would go mad. Over a year ago, when she'd agreed to come to Ireland with Daddy, she'd been under the impression that he would just pick up the 'kiddies', as she called us, and we'd all get on with our new life.

Jessie wasn't one to complain. She told Daddy how grateful she was for the wireless. Daddy had made it himself, and Jessie was able to get the BBC on it. She liked to listen to *Workers' Playtime*, a programme of tunes that was aired every day at lunch-time. She kept the volume low because Granddad didn't like all that 'modern muck', the new swing music that had become so popular. Daddy told her not to mind Granddad, that his bark was worse than his bite, and he asked Granddad to be a little more tolerant of Jessie. Granddad said he had no problem with Jessie and that, in fact, he quite liked her. He just didn't need a woman fussing over him.

'I've been alone since your mammy died,' he said, 'and I have managed to survive quite well, thank you very much.'

Daddy refrained from pointing out to Granddad the dreadful state of his house or the fact that he practically lived on brown bread and marmalade or that his clothes and bed linen were in need of a wash. What was the use? Daddy had other things on his mind. And he hadn't forgotten his application to the Housing Department. He hadn't been back to that dreadful office since the day he'd filled out the forms, but he had written many times, reminding them of his request. All he got in response were form letters telling him the matter was under consideration and instructing him to inform the Department immediately if there was any change in his circumstances. Despite this lack of encouragement, Daddy hoped it wouldn't be long before he got a Corporation house. And when he did, Jessie would be able to cook and clean until the cows came home.

The day Mr Conolly came to see me at the convent, the

nuns made a big fuss over my dress and my hair. Mother Bernadette didn't know why Mr Conolly wanted to see me, but she told me that I wasn't to worry because the Reverend Mother would be with me. I wasn't at all worried. I knew Mr Conolly from the day Daddy'd taken me to his office and I liked him.

Mother Bernadette led me to the Reverend Mother's office. Mr Conolly was there, drinking tea. He got up from his chair, held his enormous hand out to me, and said that it was nice to see me again.

'You're getting to be a big girl now,' he said, shaking my hand.

The Reverend Mother told me to be seated. I took a chair next to Mr Conolly so that the two of us were side by side, opposite her desk.

'Now then, child,' she said, 'Mr Conolly wants to have a few words with you. You're not to be afraid, and you must tell the truth.'

She smiled at me and I wondered if she'd forgotten my name again.

Mr Conolly began by asking me how I was 'bearing up'.

I said I didn't understand the question.

'Are you very unhappy here?' he asked.

The Reverend Mother tapped the desk with her finger and said, 'I warned you. We have spoken about the kind of questions you will ask the child.'

Mr Conolly laughed and told her he was sorry. 'I didn't mean for it to come out like that,' he said. But I could tell that he *had* meant it to come out like that, because he had a funny mischievous look in his eyes. Then he grew serious. 'How would you feel, Evelyn,' he said, 'if you couldn't go home until you were a big girl of, say, sixteen?'

I told him that I would be very sad. But I added that I wasn't worried about being kept in the convent forever.

'Daddy is going to get me out before long. There are clever men helping him, and his case is going to the Supreme Court.'

Mr Conolly nodded. He was one of the clever men. 'Do you like it here?' he asked.

I said that it was fine. I told him that I had many friends and that most of the nuns were kind to me.

'But I miss my brothers,' I said, 'and I want us all to be home with Daddy.'

Then I looked at the Reverend Mother. I didn't want to hurt her feelings, so I added that after I went home to Daddy, I could always come back and visit everyone.

The Reverend Mother said, 'Tell the gentleman what you have learned since you've come to stay with us.'

'I can knit socks on four needles and feed the chickens and boil the mash for the pigs,' I said proudly.

'I see,' Mr Conolly said. 'And what other work do you do?' He put a special emphasis on 'work'.

'Sometimes I work in the laundry and sometimes in the boot room,' I said.

'Ah. And I suppose you get very tired, do you, darling?'

The Reverend Mother warned him again. She said she would terminate the interview if he kept on this way. I told Mr Conolly that I didn't get tired.

'But I get a headache when Mother Paul makes me go to choir practice,' I said.

Mr Conolly nodded and gave me a smile. 'Well, my dear,' he said, 'have courage. And say a prayer for our team.' Then he turned to the Reverend Mother. 'Don't worry. I'm finished now. I've heard all I want to hear.'

He thanked me for taking the time to talk to him. The Reverend Mother rang her little bell and Mother Bernadette appeared almost immediately to take me back to my classroom down the hall.

Mr Conolly reported back to Daddy and Nick and Mr Beatty. He said that he doubted I would be much help in gaining the judges' sympathy.

'She desperately misses her brothers and wants to be home with you, Desmond, but she clearly enjoys life in the convent. It could be,' he added, 'that she's making the best of things. Children are resilient. But getting her to make a statement seems to me rather risky.'

It was agreed that I shouldn't make a statement after all. The four men discussed instead the possibility of the judges interviewing me in their chambers. Mr Conolly thought that was a risk too, but Daddy argued that I should be interviewed. He remembered how sad I'd been to have to go to the convent and how I'd come to life when I'd seen the boys in Kilkenny. He felt that, if given the chance, I would be very clear about wishing to be back among my family.

After much debating, the men agreed with Daddy.

Before he left that night, Daddy raised a question no one but he seemed concerned with.

'I don't know how I'm going to pay for all this,' he said.

'Don't worry yourself, Desmond,' Mr Conolly said. 'It's *pro bono*. In other words, we aren't doing this for the money.'

*

With only a week to go before the Supreme Court was due to sit, Mr Conolly received a letter from the Minister, asking to see him. Mr Conolly agreed and made an appointment for four o'clock the following Thursday. He told Daddy about the letter and said that he had a fair idea of why the Minister should want a private meeting with him at this stage in the proceedings.

'I suspect Mulcahy's going to offer you a deal,' he said. 'Under Section 69 of the Children Act, he can order a conditional release of Evelyn. My guess is that he'll do that, with the proviso that he can recall her at whatever time he sees fit. That time, of course, would be when all the attention dies down. At which point, we'd have to begin the whole process again, from scratch.'

SIX

Daddy didn't say anything for a minute. It sounded to him like the first bit of light in what had been a dark eighteen months. He was sick of the fight. Jessie wasn't going to last much longer living with Granddad, and he was worried about the boys. They were getting so used to their lives at the convent in Kilkenny, and the younger ones seemed to have no memory at all of the flats or of ever having been part of a family.

He worried about me too. Hadn't Mr Conolly told him that I was happy at the convent? Our partings weren't as painful to me as they'd been in the beginning, and this hadn't escaped Daddy's notice. I would wave goodbye cheerfully, and Daddy would watch me skipping back to my friends as he pulled away. He thought I was getting very 'holy', too, and he didn't like that. All these things were running through Daddy's mind as he thought about what Mr Conolly had said. He was starting to fear he would lose us forever, and a crumb was better than no loaf at all.

'If Mulcahy offers a deal,' he said to Mr Conolly, 'I'll take it. At least I'll have the children with me, and he'd have a hell of a time trying to get his hands on them again. To tell you the truth, TJ, I don't know if I can take another week in court. All the bloody nonsense. And, don't forget, there's a good chance we won't win. Take whatever he offers,' he said.

Daddy got up to go.

'Sit down. There's something you should know. I'm almost certain he will only offer to release Evelyn. I doubt very much he'll let the boys go. And what's more, we will have to agree not to pursue the matter any further. Desmond,' he said, 'we've come too far to give up now. Reconsider. I'm sure we can win this case.'

Daddy shook his head.

'Look,' Mr Conolly continued, 'Mulcahy must think we have a fairly good chance of winning or he wouldn't be asking to see me. Do you know how many children are locked up in these so-called schools, in situations far worse than those your children are in? Think, man, think.'

Daddy said that he wasn't interested in changing the world. He just wanted us all back together again so we could get on with our lives. If other people benefited from the attention the case generated, well and good. But he didn't give a curse for anyone else's problems; they could solve them themselves.

'If he offers to release Evelyn *and* the boys,' he said, 'I want you to accept.'

Mr Conolly continued to argue with Daddy, trying to convince him to carry on with the case. After the High Court hearing, Daddy had given up on his 'kidnap' plan, but only temporarily. Now, sitting in Mr Conolly's office, he knew that if he lost in the Supreme Court, he was going to take us out of Ireland, one way or another. He said nothing about this to Mr Conolly, of course. He would discuss it with Jessie later. But if he could get his children back without having to either go through the Supreme Court or escape to England, he would do it. In the end,

Daddy stuck to his decision: if the Minister agreed to release all of us, they would do a deal. If he would let only me go, they would refuse.

'When will I know what's happened at the meeting?' Daddy asked.

'Ring me around six on Thursday.'

Daddy left Mr Conolly's office that day with a great weight on his shoulders. He was only thirty-one, but he felt like an old man. The days of Strawberry Beds seemed like another age.

The first time Daddy'd become a father, he'd been over-joyed. He was so excited, in fact, that the men at work gave him stick about it. Joe Conlan, a humourless old painter who'd worked alongside Daddy when Daddy was still a journeyman, had remarked one day when Daddy was faithfully reporting every 'dribbly coo and toothless smile' of his baby daughter, 'Sure, you'd think she was the first babbie ever born.'

Joe found the chat about babies boring and said he went to work to get away from all that. At last count, his missus has produced nine, and now her belly was swollen with another. 'And they're all the bloody same to me,' he said, 'gobs open at one end and shite coming out the other. Aye, lad, you'll be well over the novelty by the time she's on her sixth.'

With that, he'd sloshed the dregs of his billycan across the yard and stomped off to have his roll-up in peace. Mick, the foreman, told Daddy not to mind Joe. He said that Joe had a hard time trying to feed all those mouths and that Joe's missus was forever nagging him to do more overtime.

'Aye, if the fecking Church helped to feed the babbies they're always preaching at us to have, life would be a bed of roses, I'm sure.'

Daddy'd reflected on Joe's jaundiced view of babies and decided to limit his family to three. Of course, it hadn't worked out that way. After the third baby, Daddy's alarm had increased with every new pregnancy. But he loved his last three children as much as his first three and, come hell or high water, he would get every one of them back.

After his meeting with Mr Conolly, Daddy headed to work. They were painting new Corporation houses on the north side of Dublin. He was worried that when this job finished, he'd be laid off again. It was already the beginning of October, and the cold, wet winter was closing in. The bad weather would last at least into February, and building work would grind to a halt until spring.

Daddy's workmates persuaded him to go for a few jars after their shift that day. Con Reilly, one of the old hands, took the money from his pay packet and carefully divided it in two, as he did each week, slipping one half into his top pocket and patting his chest.

'That's for my mot,' he said, meaning his wife.

The other half he kept for his 'bit of sport'. Every week, he'd find a Pitch and Toss game in some back alley and lose every penny of his half of the wages. Ever the optimist, Con would then dip into the mot's half until that was gone too, leaving him begging the men for the lend of a few bob until Thursday. All the men knew that they would never see the few bob again, but Con was a good skin and agreeable company, and they considered their loans to him part of their weekly entertainment costs. Sometimes poor Con appeared on Monday morning with a black eye, and when anyone asked him where he'd got the shiner, he'd say.

'A fecking lamp post jumped out at me, honest to God!'

The convent was buzzing. Every corner of it was getting scrubbed and polished. The women from the penitentiary were helping. They were dotted around the place on ladders, washing windows and paintwork. The nuns told us not to be annoying them – in other words, to keep away from them. But the women from the pen had great craic together and were such a laugh that we tried to be in their company as often as we could. I heard words I'd never heard before, and instinct told me not to repeat them in front of the nuns. Old Joe rushed about on his stumpy legs, painting anything that didn't move and roaring at whoever came within three yards of him.

'Keep your mitts off the paint job!'

Anyone who asked the nuns what all the cleaning was about was told, 'Not now, child.'

Mother Paul was more cantankerous than usual, and even sweet, gentle Mother Imelda had a worried look on her face as she climbed up and down a little ladder, shining the statues in the long hall.

We found out what was going on. The School Inspectors were coming to see us, along with the Minister for Education and the Bishop. A reporter from the *Evening Press* was coming too, and he was going to take photographs.

When the great day arrived, we were all lined up along

the drive and told to wave and cheer when the motorcars pulled up to the door. A few of the bigger girls were given new uniforms and new shoes and instructed to stand at the front door with some of the nuns, to welcome our guests. I was told to stand beside Mother Bernadette.

When we were all in place, two huge black cars swept into the drive, with a Gardai motorbike leading them. Several men got out of the cars. The nuns kissed the Bishop's ring, and the Reverend Mother shook hands with an important-looking man in a dark suit who smiled broadly as he looked over the line of nuns and girls. The photographer took a lot of pictures and called, 'This way, Minister,' and 'Smile, girls.'

The nuns sent me up to the sewing room to stay with Mother Teresa so that my picture would not be taken with the Minister. I didn't know at the time why they'd sent me to the sewing room. I didn't even know this was the same Minister Daddy was fighting in court.

When we went to the refectory at tea time, we got quite a shock. The tables were covered with white tablecloths. On top of the tables was a feast of lovely fancy-cut sandwiches, cakes and pots of tea. We could hardly believe that any of this was meant for us, and we hesitated before we took our seats. The Reverend Mother and the eminent visitors were at the top table, along the far wall. This was another first; the Reverend Mother never ate in the refectory with us. In fact, we'd never imagined her eating anywhere. Or using the lav, for that matter.

Daddy was sitting in Mr Conolly's office. Mr Conolly was telling him about his meeting with the Minister.

'He's offering to let you have Evelyn but only on the condition that he can recall her at any time. And, the boys stay where they are in Kilkenny. It's a bit of a blow, all right, though it's what we expected.'

Daddy didn't say anything.

'So it's off to court we go,' he said. 'I will see you on Tuesday.'

Daddy was up early and got dressed carefully in his best suit and overcoat on the first day of the Supreme Court. He wore the new brown brogues that Granddad had bought him for the occasion. Jessie handed him his trilby hat as he left the house. She told him to be brave.

Granddad said he'd be down at the court later on. 'And remember,' he said, 'what's for you won't go by you.'

Daddy met Mr Beatty just inside the Four Courts. The entrance hall was a massive, circular area with a domed roof. The courts themselves were located off the circle, like spokes. It seemed to Daddy that there were hundreds of people milling about, but he could still hear his own footsteps echoing as he walked. When he looked towards the Chancery courtroom, where his case would be heard, he saw that a queue of reporters had already formed.

'It's an important case, Desmond,' Mr Beatty said. 'You could be making legal history here this week.'

Daddy heard a voice he recognised behind him, calling his name. When he turned around, he saw Mrs Sullivan pushing her way over to him.

'Ah Dessie, I had to come,' she said. 'I've been praying for you since I heard about the case. Tell me, how are the babbies?'

She prattled on, but Daddy wasn't passing much heed of her. A number of reporters had spotted him and were making a beeline in his direction. They all started firing questions at once. Daddy didn't know which way to turn. Mr Beatty stepped in and pushed him past the reporters and towards the barristers' chambers. He told the reporters that they would be issuing a statement later that day and that Daddy would be happy to answer their questions then. One of the reporters wondered if they really expected to win. He said this was a David and Goliath case, and he asked Mr Beatty what they were going to use for a slingshot.

'Right is might,' Mr Beatty said, and added that they were confident of a resounding victory over archaic and draconian laws.

At exactly ten o'clock, an official called for order in the court and told everyone to be upstanding.

A hush fell over the room. Five justices filed in from a side door and took their seats at the head of the court. Behind them on the wall was a large plaque with the Irish Harp on it, the official symbol of Ireland. Chief Justice Maguire sat in the centre of the other justices and all five men looked down from what seemed to Daddy a great height. The justices wore black gowns and short white wigs and appeared extremely solemn. Each one had a thick pink file. They opened their files and started studying them, looking for all the world as though they had never set eyes on them before.

Mr Conolly and Nick, who were also wearing black gowns and wigs, sat at a table facing the bench. Mr Conolly's unruly grey curls escaped from under his wig, making it look as though the wig had just happened to land on top of his head. The counsel for the State was seated at a table a few feet away. The proceedings began when Mr Kenny, the Minister's senior counsel, got to his feet and began his opening argument. He reminded the court that the case was 'solely a matter of the validity of the statute under which Evelyn Doyle is being detained.'

The previous court hearings were then reviewed, along with the grounds on which Daddy's counsel had been granted the right to appeal the High Court's decision. The various letters were detailed that had passed between the Minister and Daddy's counsel since the time Daddy had first written to request my release over a year ago. Mr Conolly and Nick scribbled furiously on their thick yellow pads. Daddy wondered what they could be writing about because they seemed to be taking down more words than were actually being spoken. Daddy listened as the State's counsel recounted the events of the day Mammy left.

A voice from the public gallery said, 'The Devil take the bitch'. He was sure it was Mrs Sullivan. There were murmurs from the public gallery of, 'It's a disgrace', and, 'Give the man his child.'

A court official called for order and the Chief Justice said that if there were any more interruptions, he would clear the court. Daddy wished he would clear the court right then, but Mr Beatty told him this was just what they needed.

'With the people on our side, the papers will be sympathetic,' he whispered.

Daddy noticed that Granddad wasn't in the public

gallery. Later, he found out that Granddad had tried to get in but had been turned away by the usher, who told him that there was no more room. When Granddad explained that he was Mr Doyle's father, the usher guided him into the press section and found him a seat at the end of a row. From where he sat, Granddad could just see the back of Daddy's head and was alarmed to notice, for the first time, that Daddy's hair was turning grey. He hoped that Daddy wasn't going to take after his own Uncle Francis, whose hair had gone white in his early thirties. Uncle Francis had been a priest. No one noticed how eccentric he was getting until he was found running down O'Connell Street stark naked. Granddad's mammy said she would die of the shame of it, her own brother in a lunatic asylum. Granddad had been praying that all this business with the courts wouldn't turn his son's brain funny, and there were times he thought it might be best to leave us in the convents, where we could come to no harm, as long as he and Daddy could visit often. Daddy would get annoyed with Granddad when he talked like that.

'Every time I leave them there,' he said, 'it's like the first time. I can't bear to look at their little faces. And how do I know what they're thinking? The boys would never forgive me if I let the Bastard Brothers have them, and I'd never forgive myself.'

Granddad understood, but he also believed that loving anyone brought unbearable pain. In his experience, anyway.

Mr Kenny was addressing the court again. He read Articles 41 and 42 of the Constitution, both of which referred to 'the Family'. Article 41 held that the family had 'inalienable and imprescriptible rights' and guaranteed that the State would protect the family in its 'constitution and authority'. Article 42 stated that the family was 'the primary and natural educator of the child'.

Mr Conolly turned to his team and said, 'I know where he's going with this one.'

Mr Kenny continued, raising the question of what exactly constituted a 'family'.

'Is "family" a philosophical concept here?' he asked. 'Or is it a physical congregation of individuals living within four walls?'

Mr Conolly got to his feet and interrupted Mr Kenny.

'With due respect, Your Honours, surely what we're here to argue is the validity of Section 10 of the Children Act, and whether or not it is repugnant to the Constitution.'

The Chief Justice conferred with his four colleagues, then said, 'Is it not a matter to be considered, whether the case here should not have been opened by Mr Conolly?'

The five justices conferred again.

'Surely,' the Chief Justice said, 'it would be more helpful to the court to have the unconstitutionality argued by the party interested in maintaining that unconstitutionality. We are all, therefore, of the opinion that it would be logical for Mr Conolly to argue the matter first. We will adjourn until ten o'clock tomorrow morning, to enable Mr Conolly to prepare his opening arguments.'

Everyone stood up, and the justices filed out.

Mr Conolly told Nick that they were in for a long night. He looked at Daddy and said that he hadn't time to discuss anything at the moment and hoped he understood. He suggested that Daddy go outside the Four Courts and

make friends with the hacks from the press. Mr Beatty
gathered his papers from the table. As he walked with
Daddy out of the courtroom, he asked, 'Have you ever
read the Constitution, Des?'

Daddy shook his head.

'Not many have,' he said. 'Did you know, for example,
that an Irish man cannot accept a knighthood from the
Queen of England without the Irish government's permission? That's a strange thing to put in a constitution, don't
you think?'

As soon as they came through the front door of the Four
Courts, they were met by a horde of reporters and camera-
men, all shouting and snapping photographs. Mr Beatty
answered a few questions, then promised two or three of
the men that they could go with Daddy the next time he
visited me in the convent.

When they'd got free of the crowd, he asked Daddy if
he'd like to go for lunch. Daddy said no, that he had
something he had to do and didn't have much time.

Mr Beatty waved goodbye, and Daddy walked back
towards Church Street, where he'd parked the car. He
found Granddad waiting for him. Granddad was leaning
against a wall, smoking a Sweet Afton. He had his coat
buttoned to the neck and had turned the collar up to protect his ears from the cold wind that was blowing.

Instead of heading towards Granddad's house, Daddy
drove south and across O'Connell Bridge.

'Where are you taking me?' Granddad asked.

'We're going to the National Library,' Daddy said.
'We're going to trawl through every word of the Irish
Constitution. Will you help me?'

They arrived at the library on Kildare Street just after two o'clock. The man behind the desk was a little surprised by their request; he said he'd never been asked for the Constitution before. Daddy told him he wanted two copies.

'In English, if you don't mind.'

Granddad said no, he wanted his copy in Irish. 'It might be slightly different from the English version,' he said to Daddy. 'You don't know.'

The two of them spent the rest of the afternoon at the library, reading and taking notes. They didn't even slip outside for a smoke. The librarian was looking at his watch and finding all sorts of excuses to walk past their table; he wasn't used to men like this sitting in the library all day. He coughed politely, and Granddad told him they wouldn't be much longer.

'Give us a chance, son,' he said. 'This is very important.' He waved his hand at the man to dismiss him and went back to his task.

They pored over the two Constitutions until their eyes were swimming. Finally, Daddy said, 'That's it! I've got it! Look at this, Dad.'

He showed Granddad a phrase contained in Article 42. Granddad agreed that this seemed to be an important point that was relevant to the case, and Daddy carefully copied it out. It referred to the State, under certain circumstances, supplying the place of the parents, *'but always with due regard for the natural and imprescriptible rights of the child.'* Daddy couldn't remember his legal team ever having mentioned anything about the children's rights. He handed the documents back to the librarian and pressed five shillings into his hand, thanking him for staying on nearly an hour past closing time.

Daddy had to push his way slowly through the courthouse foyer the following morning, it was crowded. People insisted on shaking his hand and wishing him luck. A reporter tagged along beside him and asked him questions. Mindful of Mr Conolly's advice to think carefully about what he said to the press, he decided to say nothing. An usher spotted him and came to his rescue, escorting him through the throng and into the courtroom. Mr Conolly was already seated with Nick. Daddy passed Mr Conolly a folded sheet of paper, on which he'd written down the section from the Constitution. But Mr Conolly didn't get a chance to look at it, because just then, the usher called for order and the five justices made their way to the bench.

Justice Lavery addressed Mr Conolly.

'Would not an order by the Minister under Section 69 of the Children Act end this case, Mr Conolly?'

Mr Conolly conferred with Nick, then replied to the bench.

'It would, Your Honour, but it would leave a judgment of the High Court impeaching the validity of the statute in question.'

Mr Kenny got to his feet.

'The Minister has already agreed to an order under Section 69 to accommodate the release of the child,' he said, 'but his offer has been refused by Mr Doyle's counsel.'

'It was a conditional release,' Mr Conolly shot back, 'and not in my client's best interests.'

The Chief Justice indicated that Mr Conolly should proceed with his argument. Mr Conolly read out Section 10 of the Children Act. He allowed that the High Court had indeed correctly applied the statute as it stood.

'However,' he said, 'I submit that this statute constitutes an invasion of the parental rights guaranteed by the Constitution, as it contains provisions which have resulted in the detention of the child in a State industrial school against the wishes of her father.'

Mr Conolly paused to take a sip of water. He was beginning to enjoy himself. Nick whispered to Daddy that there would be no stopping him now.

'In his heyday, TJ could persuade anyone that black was white.' Nick smiled to himself and continued taking notes.

Justice Lavery addressed Mr Conolly. 'It is unnecessary to make further reference to previous court submissions,' he said. 'Nor is it necessary to refer to the question of whether or not the father alone had the right to remove the child from the school. The point we are debating is whether the statute that prevented him from doing so is unconstitutional.'

Justice Kingsmill-Moore spoke. 'It is clear that this is a case of *casus omissus*,' he said.

Daddy asked Nick what *casus omissus* meant.

'It's a case not provided for by the statute,' Nick said. 'In other words, the legislators didn't think a case like this would ever come up.'

The bench seemed to be in sympathy with Daddy's counsel, and Mr Conolly sounded increasingly confident.

'Two down, three to go,' Nick whispered to Daddy.

Mr Conolly read out the relevant articles of the Constitution as well as selected sections of the Children Act, attempting to force the Court to admit that Section 10 was 'repugnant' to the Constitution and, therefore, invalid.

Daddy listened carefully as the second day of the hearings dragged on, thinking about the slip of paper he'd handed to Mr Conolly that morning.

All the girls from my dormitory were lined up outside the bathroom, waiting to get their hair and nails trimmed by Mother Imelda and Mother Bernadette. When my turn came, I begged Mother Imelda to cut my hair, which was down to my waist, but she wouldn't hear of it. I wanted to be like all the other girls.

'No, no, pet,' she said, 'you know I can't cut your hair. You might be going home soon, and what would your Daddy say if he arrived and your lovely long hair was gone?'

With that, she shooed me out of the bathroom. After the nuns were finished with all the girls and had gone downstairs again, I turned to Siobhán.

'Will you cut my hair?'

'Oh, no,' she said, 'Mother Bernie would skin me alive.'

I begged her. I told her that I wouldn't let on who had done it. But she still refused.

'All right,' I said, 'I suppose I'll have to do it myself then.'

I got the scissors from the bathroom, and the other girls gathered round. Just as I was about to make the first cut, Siobhán shrieked, 'Jaysus, Evelyn! Don't do it.'

She took the scissors from me. She blessed herself three times, then looked at my head from various angles, trying to decide where to start. Her hand was shaking, and some of the girls were saying, 'Ooooh.' Siobhán told them to keep their gobs shut. I watched the long blonde tresses piling up on the floor. When Siobhán had finished, my hair reached to just below my ears. I was delighted. I didn't give a second thought to what Daddy would say when he saw me.

After we'd swept the floor, we went down for our tea. All the girls were excited about my new hair, but when Mother Bernadette saw me, she nearly screamed. 'Evelyn Doyle! Who cut your hair?'

I refused to tell her. Then I said that I'd done it myself. She didn't believe me but I stuck to my story.

As I undressed for bed that night I saw strands of hair on the floor, and I thought of the time Mammy and Daddy had had the awful fight over Mammy's hair.

Daddy'd come home from work one night in bad humour, and Mammy'd told us all to be very quiet. She put his dinner of mashed potato, sausages and peas on the table and sat down by the fire to read her book.

Daddy started eating, but then he let out at a roar at Mammy.

'What the feck is this!'

He pulled a long black hair from his mashed potato.

Mammy said, 'It looks to me like a hair.' She told him she didn't know how it had got into his dinner.

'Well, bring me a new plate,' Daddy said. But Mammy said there wasn't any more dinner, and Daddy started shouting about 'a working man not being able to get a decent bit of dinner'. He went on and on about the hair.

'Shut up, will you?' Mammy said. 'It's only a bloody hair.'

Daddy wouldn't let it go. I was sitting in the big chair with a couple of the boys. We were watching, not saying a word. We could see that there was going to be a fight. But we were shocked by what Mammy did next.

She stomped off to the bedroom and, when she came back out, she had her hairbrush in her hand. Daddy was reading his paper, which was propped up against a milk bottle, and his dinner was still in front of him on the table. Mammy put a finger to her lips to shush us, then tiptoed up behind Daddy. She leaned over his shoulder and tossed her hair forward, brushing it over his dinner plate.

'Now you've got a bloody hair in your dinner,' she said. 'In fact, you have lots of bloody hairs in your dinner!'

Then she threw the brush down and grabbed her coat from where it was hung on the nail by the front door and ran out of the flat. Daddy sat staring at his plate and said nothing. Mammy had never done anything like that before. We all started laughing, but we soon stopped. Daddy was in a terrible temper, and he stormed off to his bedroom.

When we went to bed that night, Mammy still hadn't come home. The next morning, though, she was sitting in her usual place by the fire, as if nothing at all had happened.

In the dormitory, I picked the strands of hair off the floor and threw them down the toilet in the bathroom. I didn't think about our life in the flat much any more but, for a moment anyway, I missed it. And I wondered what Mammy would have thought of my short hair.

After court adjourned on the second day of the hearings, Daddy arrived at the convent with Mr Conolly, Mr Beatty, Nick, and five or six men from the newspapers. The nuns dressed me in nice new clothes. Mother Teresa said that I was going to have my photograph in the papers.

'You must smile for Ireland, dear,' she said, and tied one of my green ribbons on top of my head.

When Daddy saw my short hair, he got a shock. He was about to lay into Mother Bernadette, but I told him that I'd cut it myself.

He shook his head, called me a bold girl, and said, 'Well, I suppose it will grow again.'

I knew that if the men from the newspaper hadn't been there, there'd have been holy war.

We spent the next hour going round the grounds of the convent, taking photographs. I found it very exciting. I didn't get a chance to ask Daddy what was happening in court, but the reporters seemed to think he was winning. One of them asked if Daddy intended to take his five sons home when he took me home.

Daddy said that when he got a bigger house, he would get the boys too.

With all these people around, I felt shy and couldn't think of anything to say to Daddy. When a reporter asked me if I was looking forward to going home, I just stared at the ground and didn't answer.

Instead, I said, 'Daddy, I like your new brown shoes.'

Daddy smiled. He told me that he had to go to Mr Conolly's office now but that he'd be back to see me very soon.

'Things are going well for us, pet, but it's not over yet. Sit tight and say a prayer for Mr Conolly, that he can win for us.'

In that evening's paper, much to Daddy's embarrassment, it was reported that I liked his new brown shoes.

After Daddy left the convent, he went to Mr Conolly's office, where Mr Conolly and Nick were discussing the American Constitution.

'What has the American Constitution to do with our case?' he asked.

'Well,' Nick said, 'the Irish Constitution is, to a degree, based on it. And we think that some amendments to the American Constitution may apply to your case. Do you see where we're headed?'

Daddy said he was in favour of anything that would help the case, but he hoped that they weren't going to offend the justices by introducing the American Constitution into their arguments.

'The Fourteenth Amendment to the US Constitution grants and protects the civil liberties of all US citizens,' Mr Conolly explained. 'In a nutshell, it says that no State in America may pass laws depriving any person born or naturalized in the country of equal protection under the law. Nor can it deprive them of their property, liberty or life without due process of law. Now,' Mr Conolly continued, 'these are principles that apply to your daughter. She has committed no crime, and yet she has been deprived of her liberty. She's being detained against her will. Not to mention yours.'

Daddy listened closely, hoping they were on the right track.

'What about the section I found the other night in the library?' he asked.

'We'll use it,' Mr Conolly said. 'But that alone might not be enough.'

They discussed their tactics for the following day and convinced themselves that they were ready for anything the Minister's team could throw at them. Daddy wasn't so sure. Events had a nasty habit of biting your arse, just when you least expected them to, and he wasn't going to believe in any victory until it had actually come to pass.

As he drove home, though, he realised that he'd begun to feel a little more optimistic.

He stopped at a newsagent's on Dorset Street to buy cigarettes. Even though he'd been with the photographers at the convent that day, he was still shocked to see a picture of us on the front of several copies of the *Evening Press* laid out on the counter.

Daddy handed the man behind the counter his money and put the Sweet Aftons in his coat pocket.

As the man gave Daddy his change, he said, 'Don't I know you from somewhere?'

Daddy said, 'No, I don't think so.'

The man persisted, naming places he had been to or lived in and asking Daddy whether he knew the places. Daddy could see out of the corner of his eye his own face on the counter, and he wondered how long it would take the man to recognize him.

He shook his head again. 'I'm sure you don't know me,' he said, laughing, and walked out of the shop.

When Daddy arrived for the third day of the hearings, the crowd of photographers and well-wishers had already gathered. Strangers shouted their good wishes and blessings. Men slapped him on the back as he headed towards the front door, and a woman pushed a miraculous medal into his hand. Daddy tried to take it in his stride. He wasn't exactly growing comfortable with the attention, but at least he knew what to expect now.

The proceedings opened with the officer of the court reading through the main points that had been argued over the last two days. Justice O'Dálaigh called on Nick.

'Your Honours,' Nick said, getting to his feet. 'As you know, the Irish Constitution is based on the format of the United States Constitution. The US Supreme Court has, in a long line of decisions, recognized that marriage, procreation and parent/child relationships involve fundamental rights of the kind protected by the US Constitution. They have also recognized that these rights are given equally to each individual.'

The five justices were taking notes feverishly, and the Minister's barristers were scanning thick law books. Mr Conolly gazed serenely at the bench. Nick was slowly and deliberately going through the documents before him to drive home his points.

'I refer you to the Fourteenth Amendment to the United States Constitution, in particular to Section 1, which reads: "All persons born or naturalized in the United States, and subject to the jurisdiction thereof, are citizens of the United States and of the State wherein they reside. No State shall make or enforce any law which shall abridge the privileges or immunities of citizens of the United States; nor shall *any State* deprive any person of life, liberty, or property, without due process of law; nor deny to any person within its jurisdiction the equal protection of the laws."'

Mr Conolly took over, calling the justices' attention to two rulings handed down by the US Supreme Court. First, he cited *Meyer* v. *Nebraska*, 1923. He explained that, in this case, the Court had ruled that the liberty protected by the Fourteenth Amendment included the right of the individual to engage in the common occupations of life, including marrying, establishing a home, and bringing up children. Further, Mr Conolly pointed out, the Supreme Court referred in its ruling to the 'natural duty of the parent to give his children education'.

Mr Conolly also outlined the safeguards that had been put in place in American law to protect children from abusive, criminal, or mentally unstable fathers, and reminded the Court that Daddy fell into none of these categories.

Daddy was a little nervous on hearing this, as he remembered his behaviour at the Children's Court nearly two years ago. He hoped those outbursts wouldn't qualify him as 'mentally unstable'. At the time, he'd been mad with worry. Surely if the scene were to be mentioned now, the justices would understand the agony he'd been going through, watching strangers take his children away. He could still remember the look on Noel's face – it was like a little light had gone out inside of the boy.

Mr Conolly then referred to the US Supreme Court's

ruling in *Pierce* v. *Society of the Sisters of the Holy Names of Jesus and Mary*. In this case, the Court ruled against the state 'unreasonably interfering with the liberty of parents and guardians to direct the upbringing and education of children under their control.'

'Based on these American precedents,' he said, 'as well as on Article 42 of our own Constitution, which also safeguards the right of parents to provide for their children's education, I submit to the Court that the Children Act of 1941 is repugnant to the Irish Constitution.'

With that, Mr Conolly took his seat.

At the adjacent table, there was much shuffling of papers and whispering among the Minister's counsel. Mr Conolly began jotting something down on his pad. When Daddy looked over his shoulder, he saw that his counsel was drawing a wicked caricature of Mr Kenny, in which Mr Kenny was sweating and looking thunder-struck and diving for cover under the table. Mr Conolly folded the paper and handed it to a court usher who, in turn, handed it to Mr Kenny. Mr Conolly looked over and gave a little wave, and Mr Kenny bowed his head and smiled.

Daddy was not amused by this carry-on. As far as he was concerned, whoever wasn't on your side was the enemy, and you surely didn't make jokes with him.

When court adjourned that morning, Mr Conolly explained to him that he and the Minister's counsel weren't enemies.

'We're just doing our jobs,' he said. 'Next week, we could be working on the same team. But,' he added, 'that's not to say that we both won't use every trick in the book, and a few that aren't in the book, to win this case.'

*

Court was not reconvening until two o'clock. Daddy drove back to Granddad's house. Jessie made him his favourite dinner of pork chops.

Every so often, since the day the Children's Court had taken us away, Daddy would say, 'Why me?' To which Granddad would reply, 'Why not you?'

Granddad told him that everyone had a cross, or more than one, to bear, and he often quoted the line, 'There is no greater sorrow than to recall in our misery the times when we were happy.' He said that this was a good thing to remember, and he told Daddy that he shouldn't dwell on the way things used to be but should think about the future instead.

In the afternoon, Daddy was back in court. Mr Kenny was speaking.

'The view I take,' he said, 'is that the matter before this Court has been properly stated in the High Court. Articles 41 and 42 do not confer rights on a single parent so long as both parents are alive. With the Court's permission, I cite the Tilson case of 1951 and the Frost case of 1947, heard in this Court, both of which concern parents' rights with regard to the education of their children.'

Mr Kenny continued, speaking at greater length about these cases and the decisions handed down in each.

'Any guaranteed right given to the parents was given to them jointly by the Irish Constitution. Just four years ago, this Court, in its wisdom, upheld this guarantee, determining that those rights are exercisable only by the parents jointly so long as they are both alive, as is the case here.'

Mr Conolly let out a long sigh. Judging by his expression, Daddy thought, things were taking a turn for the worse. Nick was rapidly turning the pages of a law book. Daddy asked him what was going on, and Nick said he'd explain it to him in a minute.

Mr Conolly requested an adjournment to consider the issues Mr Kenny had introduced, and court was adjourned.

Daddy left the building with Nick and Mr Conolly. They were met by the press, firing their usual round of questions. Mr Conolly told them that the fight was far from over. A radio reporter pushed a microphone under his nose, and Mr Conolly brushed it aside, but not before he'd said, 'We've a few more cards yet to play, gentlemen.'

Then the reporter asked Daddy if he would like to appeal to his wife to come forward and put an end to all this. He said that Daddy could make the appeal on his radio programme.

Daddy was shocked by the man's suggestion and nearly lost his temper right there on the steps of the Four Courts. Mr Conolly stopped him in time and, leaning back towards the microphone, told the reporter that Mrs Doyle had left the country and all efforts to trace her had failed. Then he and Nick nudged Daddy ahead of them and out into the street, where Nick flagged a taxi.

'What the feck went wrong in there today?' Daddy demanded to know, when they were back in Mr Conolly's office.

Mr Conolly told him to calm down. He handed him a large neat whiskey.

'They were trying to prove that a precedent had been established in two previous Supreme Court rulings,' he said. 'But your case differs in important ways from those Kenny referred to. It was a minor setback, Desmond, nothing more. Tomorrow we're going to come at them with everything we have, including your find from the other day. Try not to worry. We're not played out yet.'

Daddy didn't go straight home from Mr Conolly's office. He knew that the men from the press would be waiting on the doorstep. Instead, he headed out of the city, without a second thought for what Granddad or Jessie would be thinking. He drove north, with no particular destination in mind.

He stopped at Howth harbour. When he was a boy, he'd spent many Sunday mornings there with a gang of his pals. They took the tram, which crept alongside the seafront. They'd sit on the pier, their fishing lines dangling over the sea. They hardly cared if they caught anything or not. They liked just joking and talking together and setting the world to rights. If the day was warm, they'd splash around in the sea; at that age, they didn't mind the cold water. When evening came and it was getting dark, they'd rob the fields nearby for cabbages and potatoes before heading back to the Strawberry Beds.

Daddy's friend Gussie Hair-oil was always along on these raids. Gussie's mammy, Mrs Murphy, was grateful for the extra bit of food in her pantry. Mrs Murphy had known hardship all her life. She'd left school at thirteen and gone straight into service in a grand house in Dún Laoghaire, where she was at the beck and call of its masters. Every night, she fell into bed exhausted and, every morning, she was up at five o'clock, ready to begin work again.

She'd met Thomas Murphy when she was only sixteen and married him the following year. They had thirteen children together. Twelve of them contracted TB. One by one, they died, until the only surviving child was Gussie, Augustus Aloysius Thomas Murphy. That was the name his mother had given him. Back before the TB had got hold of them, Mrs Murphy'd had big plans for her children. She hadn't wanted any of them to end up with the kind of life she'd endured, and she thought that if she gave them grand names they would amount to something. She was forever choking Daddy off when he called to the house and asked if 'Gussie' could come out to play. She was even less pleased when her son earned the nickname Gussie Hair-oil.

It had started at the pictures one afternoon, in 1937. Daddy and his friends had taken the tram into the city to see *Lost Horizon*, which starred Ronald Coleman. By the time Gussie left the cinema, he had a new hero. The following day he arrived at school with his hair plastered to his skull with Brilliantine, in an imitation of Ronald Coleman. As the morning wore on and the classroom grew warmer, the oil started running down Gussie's face, much to the delight of his classmates.

When the teacher, Mr O'Gorman, finally saw what was causing all the merriment, he dragged poor Gussie by the ear out into the schoolyard and held his head under the water pump, in a vain attempt to wash the hair oil out. From that day on, Gussie was known as 'Gussie Hair-oil'.

Pud, Sniffy and Austin were also part of Daddy's gang. The boys went everywhere together, at least until they got older and, one by one, married their mots. They attended each other's weddings, where Daddy would play the piano, and they helped each other celebrate the babies, when they began to arrive.

They never got to celebrate any babies of Pud's. Not long after Pud was married, he'd fallen off a roof one day while he was at work. The four friends kept a vigil at his bedside for ten days following the accident but, early on the eleventh morning, Pud found it easier to slip away than stay and fight on and he took his last painful breath. The doctor told Ginny, his widow, that it was just as well because Pud probably would never have walked again and, more than likely, would've been a 'spastic'. Ginny said she wouldn't have cared. She'd just wanted Pud back; she hadn't even one of his babies to remember him by.

The day of the funeral, Daddy, Sniffy, Austin, and Gussie, along with Pud's Daddy and his two brothers, carried Pud's coffin through the rain.

Not long after that, Austin went to England and became a barber. Before he left, he told the others that there was a lot of money to be made in London cutting English hair.

'In this life,' he said, 'everybody has to eat, have a hair cut, and die. Therefore, there are three jobs that are guaranteed: cook, barber and undertaker.'

Sniffy agreed but said he couldn't imagine why anyone would want to be messing about with dead bodies every day, and he advised Austin to stick to the hair-cutting and cooking. But, he asked, could Austin not make just as much money cutting Irish hair? Austin punched Sniffy's shoulder and called him a 'fecking eejit' and they all had a good laugh, arguing over who had more hair, the Irish or the English.

After that, it was just Gussie and Sniffy and Daddy left in Dublin. Their time was taken up more and more by their growing broods. Daddy brought his family with him when he went fishing or, the odd time, went on his own. Occasionally, if Austin was back from England, the four of them would meet up and reminisce about the old days, but the feeling of camaraderie was gone, along with their youth.

Daddy'd grown cold, sitting on the wall there at the harbour, thinking about the things that had happened and the people that had been in his life and now were gone from it. It had got dark without his really noticing. He headed for the car and made his way back along the seafront and across the north side of the city to Granddad's house.

When he got home, he found that Jessie had been crying because it was so late and she'd had no idea where he was. Daddy never stayed out like that without letting them know beforehand. He said he was sorry and assured Jessie that he hadn't been drinking.

'I just wanted to be on my own for a bit,' he said. 'To think.'

Jessie was a little hurt that he hadn't confided in her, but she tried to understand. She was tired and wanted to sleep. Daddy hadn't eaten since lunch-time, though, and she got out some bacon and eggs. The sounds and the smells of cooking woke Granddad, and he wandered into the kitchen with the old sweaty sock wrapped round his head. Jessie told him that Daddy was in a bit of a state and needed to have some supper. Daddy had gone into the front room. He was sitting in his chair, still in his overcoat, smoking and staring into space. Granddad knocked on the door and, without waiting for an answer, went in. Sometimes this habit of Granddad's was cause for a row between him and Daddy. But Daddy hadn't much fight in him that night.

He looked at Granddad and said, 'I think we might lose tomorrow. But if we do, I'm not going to just disappear quietly. I *will* have my children back.'

Granddad told him to have his supper and get some sleep.

'You look all in, son,' he said. 'Let's see what tomorrow brings. Then we can think about what our next move should be.'

Ever since Daddy's mammy had died, when Daddy was only a boy, he and Granddad had pretty much lived their own lives and avoided interfering in each other's business. Granddad had fed and sheltered him until he was old enough to be out on his own. Beyond that, Daddy hadn't asked for much. Now, here was Granddad talking about 'our' and 'we'. It had been a long time since they'd been a 'we', not since Daddy's mammy had died. When she was still alive, he and Granddad used to get up to things together, playing little jokes on her to make her laugh. But that had come to a stop very suddenly and, until now, Daddy had almost forgotten that he and Granddad had ever been close.

Jessie brought his supper to the front room and the three of them chatted about nothing in particular while Daddy ate. If Daddy or Jessie mentioned the case, Granddad changed the subject, saying that they all needed a break, if only for an hour.

'Everything that can be done has been done,' he said, 'and it's up to the judges now and God Almighty.'

SEVEN

Daddy couldn't sleep that night. He lay in bed, watching the hands of the clock crawling towards morning. He heard Granddad get up a few times during the night and knew that he was worried too.

At six o'clock, he got out of bed and began to prepare for the day. He made a pot of tea for himself and Jessie. Granddad would make his own tea; he had a special method. He would put the teapot on the stove and let it stew until the tea was like treacle and looked thick enough to be eaten with a spoon. When he judged it to be just right, he would pour it into his large cup and sweeten it with Fussells thick, sweet condensed milk.

I adored Granddad and loved visiting him, but I dreaded it when he would say, 'Have a sup of tea, pet, it's good for the kidneys.'

He would then pour me a big cupful of the revolting brew. If he was watching, I would try to force it down but, more often than not, I found a pot plant or vase to dump it into. Fortunately, because Granddad was not a good housekeeper, he never noticed the tea congealing in strange places.

Jessie and Granddad came into the kitchen, and Granddad switched on the wireless. As the three of them ate breakfast, Daddy heard his name being mentioned. His case had been discussed on the wireless numerous times over the last few months, but this debate was particularly heated, as it was taking place on the morning of the Supreme Court's decision. Granddad turned up the volume and they listened intently. The speaker was saying what a disgrace it was that a father had to go this far just so he could bring his children home.

A second speaker, apparently representing the government, said, 'We apply the law as it stands, and this man voluntarily transferred the responsibility for his children to the State. The statute is quite clear. It's regrettable, but the Minister has to preserve the law…'

The first speaker interrupted. It was clear now that he was the presenter of the programme. 'But what law has this man, or his children, for that matter, broken? Are you telling the people of this country that six children, who are innocent of any crime, are to be locked up in institutions until they are sixteen? They don't even have the comfort of being together. What has the Church to say about this tragic situation? Father Nolan?'

Granddad started to say something, but Daddy shushed him. Up to now, the Church had mostly confined itself to commenting on the case in its own press. Now, a representative was going to speak to the general public.

'The Church's position is quite clear,' Father Nolan said. 'The sanctity of marriage is absolute, and these children's, or any child's, moral and religious wellbeing is of paramount importance. Unless and until the mother returns to the marital home, the State has the duty to ensure that the children are not returned to the father and his Protestant housekeeper.'

Daddy jumped up, knocking the chair over. His face was nearly purple with rage.

'The fecking bastards,' he roared.

Granddad tried to calm him down.

'Sit down and listen to what's being said! That's only one side talking.' Granddad was speaking to Daddy like he used to when Daddy was a boy.

They missed the last part of the priest's comments. Jessie was upset. 'Protestant' had come out sounding like a dirty word. She wasn't a particularly religious woman, but she felt insulted that she should be held responsible for putting a child, or anyone, for that matter, in moral danger. She said nothing, though. She didn't want Daddy to see how hurt she was. It would only have made him angrier and, as he was facing the final and most important day in court, she tried to settle him down.

'Dessie,' she said, 'I'm not bothered what they say about me. Let it go. The main thing is for you to be calm and in control this morning. Just ignore them.'

They turned their attention back to the wireless. But the presenter of the programme made it clear that the public was on Daddy's side.

The presenter was reading from a document. '"…with due observance of Prudence, Justice and Charity, so that the dignity and freedom of the individual may be assured…" That's a quote from the preamble to our own Constitution. Are you telling me that a person's "dignity and freedom" can be preserved only if the government and the Church decide who is entitled to that "dignity and freedom"? Where's the justice and charity in that?' he asked.

The man who was taking the government's side attempted an answer. He sounded flustered and said something about the law being applied with scrupulous fairness. The priest interrupted and repeated his line about the sanctity of marriage. The three men went round in circles a couple more times, and the programme ended with the presenter reading out a letter from a man in Sligo, who said he was in the same position Daddy was.

The letter ended, 'Tell Mr Doyle that my prayers and those of my friends and family are with him. He is a fine example of Irish courage and tenacity. God bless him, and with His help, he will triumph.'

The presenter said that he'd received hundreds of letters from ordinary citizens, many of them expressing the same views the Sligo man had.

'So we await the verdict of the Supreme Court,' he said, 'which we will be bringing to you as soon as we have it.'

Jessie began boiling pans of water to fill the large tin bath for Daddy. After the programme on the wireless, she was feeling like public enemy number one, and not for the first time since she'd come to Ireland. She wondered, yet again, if she'd made a mistake.

While Daddy was in the bath, Jessie ironed his new white shirt. She knew that his photograph would more than likely be in all the papers that night and the next morning, and she wanted him to look his best.

Granddad couldn't bear to wait at home for the verdict, and he didn't want to go to the Four Courts, with all the reporters and photographers milling about. He suggested that Jessie, or Mrs Brown, as he still called her, come with him for a drive in the country. Jessie agreed immediately. She was delighted to have the distraction and, despite her differences with Granddad, she knew that he could be soothing company.

Daddy went to Mr Conolly's office before court that day. Nick was already there, and they had their heads buried in thick law books. Mr Conolly welcomed Daddy and told him what their plan of action was.

'We're going to argue that, although both parents have an absolute right to rear their family, your wife has forfeited that right by abandoning her children.'

'What about the part my father and I found about the child's rights? Surely, you should give that a go.'

Daddy and Granddad had been excited about finding it and were sure it was relevant to the case. Mr Conolly seemed to dismiss the idea too quickly. Mr Conolly continued to insist that the whole point of the case was to establish the right of a single parent to obtain custody of his children whether or not his spouse was still living. However, he said, if things got desperate, he would introduce Daddy's find.

Nick was a little more encouraging. 'Throughout this whole case, no one has given a thought to the rights of children as citizens. Arguing that the child has rights of her own could be our trump card.'

Mr Conolly appeared to be considering it. He opened a copy of the Irish Constitution and examined it, comparing Daddy's note with the actual wording of Article 42.5.

'It says that when the State endeavours to supply the place of the parents, it must always take into account "the natural and imprescriptible rights of the child".'

'It's time to go to court,' was all he said.

They got into Mr Conolly's Humber Hawk motorcar and drove to the north side. As they approached the Four

Courts, they saw the crowd assembling. It was even bigger than it had been on the previous days, and Daddy noticed Mr Conolly's excitement.

'The wolves are circling,' the barrister said. 'Desmond, please try not to look like their dinner. Come on, smile for the birdies. Let's go to battle, boys!'

As they walked along Inns Quay towards the Four Courts, he saw a movie camera pointed at him and as they got nearer the court, he noticed the words 'Pathe News' on the side of a van parked at the kerb. Daddy tried to fall in behind Mr Conolly and Nick, but Mr Conolly told him to stay between them.

'Hold your head up, Desmond,' he said. 'You've got nothing to be ashamed of. So why hide? Just smile and leave the talking to me.'

As they drew nearer to the camera, a reporter asked Mr Conolly if he could have a few words with Daddy. Mr Conolly told the man that Daddy had nothing to say just now but that he would be happy to give an interview later in the day after they had won their case.

'Are you that confident of winning?' the reporter asked.

'Of course we're going to win, dear boy,' Mr Conolly said. 'This is the Free State of Ireland, not some Stalinist dictatorship. Now, if you'll excuse me.' Mr Conolly tipped his homburg hat, gave a little bow, and guided Daddy through the crowd.

That evening, a headline in one of the papers twisted his words: IRISH FREE STATE COMPARED TO STALINIST DICTATORSHIP.

In the foyer of the Four Courts, people cheered as Daddy was swept along towards the Chancery Court. Mr Beatty was just inside the door. He shook Daddy's hand and wished him good luck.

'I can't be with you today, Desmond. Poor Red needs me. This time, please God, they may put her away for at least a year.'

Daddy found it strange for a solicitor to be hoping that his client would be locked up, but legal men were a breed apart, as far as he could see, and the more contact he had with them the stranger they appeared.

As the courtroom grew quiet and the justices filed in, Daddy tried to read their expressions. As far as he could see, though, the faces of the five men were expressionless.

Chief Justice Maguire summed up the previous day's arguments, then asked the barristers if they were ready to proceed.

'We must conclude the matter today,' he reminded them.

Mr Conolly replied that he was more than ready, and Mr Kenny nodded. The Chief Justice invited Mr Kenny to begin.

The Minster's barrister explained that in Article 42, the Constitution had invested the State, 'as guardian of the common good', with the power to use whatever 'appropriate means' were necessary to supply the place of the parents in cases of parental failure.

Mr Conolly raised the question of who decided what sort of means were 'appropriate' in this case. 'And how,' he asked, 'is the "the common good" being served by depriving this father of his children?'

Mr Kenny continued. 'Were this case to be decided in Mr Doyle's favour, its consequences would be far-reaching.

The release by this Court of Mr Doyle's child would provide, by extension, justification for other parents to regain from the State custody of children who are either juvenile offenders or mentally unsound. Such a situation would clearly not be in the interests of the common good and would be contrary to the intention of the legislators who framed the Constitution.'

He sat down, eyeing Mr Conolly with a look that said, 'Get round that one.'

It was nearly time for the lunch recess. Nick whispered to Mr Conolly that it might be a good time to introduce the issue of the child's constitutional rights.

'Your Honours,' Mr Conolly said, rising from his seat. 'The child in question, Evelyn Doyle, has individual rights under Article 42, Subsection 5 of the Irish Constitution. This article explicitly states that a child has "natural and imprescriptible rights". I submit that no means would be appropriate which interfered with such rights.'

There were murmurs in the public gallery and much whispering among the Minister's counsel. Mr Conolly took a long drink of water, trying to appear indifferent to Mr Kenny's obvious surprise. Clearly, no one had expected the issue of the child's rights to be raised.

Mr Conolly continued. Based on the provisions of Article 42, Subsection 5, he argued that 'the child has the right to be returned to either or both parents and cannot be prevented from exercising this right.'

The court adjourned for lunch. Mr Conolly told Daddy that he felt things had swung in their favour.

'They're going to want to study this latest piece of information,' he said, clearly looking forward to the afternoon session. Daddy wanted to know if he would be able to bring me home that day.

Mr Conolly was cautious. 'It depends on how Kenny tries to get round the question of Evelyn's constitutional rights,' he said.

As they were leaving the courtroom, an usher handed Mr Conolly a note.

'Mr Kenny wants to see me in the barristers' chambers,' he said, looking at the piece of paper. 'Nick, get Desmond something to eat and order my usual. I won't be long.'

Half an hour later, Mr Conolly walked into the pub. He called for his food, which was being kept warm in the kitchen, and tucked into it with gusto.

'I have to eat. Then I'll tell you what Kenny said.'

When at last he was ready to speak, Mr Conolly said, 'They don't want the case to go any further. Kenny has offered to have Evelyn released today if we agree to not carry on with the point about the child's constitutional rights. They haven't had time to study this section of the constitution, and we've thrown them off balance by introducing it.'

Daddy was overjoyed and put his hand out to shake Mr Conolly's. But Mr Conolly didn't offer his hand.

'I didn't say that I'd accepted, Desmond. In fact, I refused. With apologies to you, we must take this case to its conclusion.'

Daddy was furious and demanded to know why Mr Conolly had not consulted him.

'I have the intelligence to make decisions that affect my own family.'

Mr Conolly said that he understood Daddy's anger.

'But,' he added, 'once again, there was no mention of the boys. It was a decision that had to be made on the spot, and the long-term implications needed to be weighed against the immediate benefits. Remember, Desmond, this case is not just about you any more.'

Daddy was still angry, but he began to calm down. He didn't want a conditional release any more than he had the first time it was offered. He asked what was likely to happen in the afternoon.

'It all depends on the judges,' Mr Conolly said.

Daddy was hoping for a more promising reply, but he knew there was nothing he could do but wait.

There was tension in the courtroom as Mr Kenny opened the proceedings after the lunch recess. He stood before the court, saying nothing for several seconds, which only made Daddy's nerves worse.

'I would remind the court once again,' he said finally, 'of the consequences of invalidating Section 10 of the Children Act...'

Another long pause.

Then: 'Beyond that, I have nothing further to submit.'

He bowed to the bench and sat down.

Mr Conolly rose.

'Both parents in concert have an absolute right with regard to the rearing of their children. However, in this case, only one parent is concerned, and his position is no weaker than if he were making the application for his daughter's release jointly. This is not a case of conflict between parents; the mother has abandoned the family. I also remind the Court of the child's rights as guaranteed by the Constitution. I submit that the Children Act is repugnant to the Constitution because it deprives the father of, *inter alia*, his right to direct his children's education.'

Mr Conolly bowed to the Court and took his seat.

Daddy felt himself relax slightly. His barrister's argument sounded compelling, and he allowed himself to imagine that he might be only an hour or two from taking me home.

The Chief Justice spoke. He went over the salient points of the case and the arguments put forth over the last few days by both the Minister's and Daddy's counsel. He complimented both sides on their gentlemanly conduct. Daddy wished that he would just come to the point; he felt like shouting, 'Get on with it!'

'However...' the Chief Justice said.

Mr Conolly groaned at the sound of 'however'. He'd once told Daddy that you could guess which way a decision was headed by the number of 'howevers' you heard.

The Chief Justice looked at him from the bench, and Mr Conolly bowed his head in apology for the interruption.

Keeping his eyes on Mr Conolly, he continued.

'*However*, the matter of the Constitution is one that requires careful consideration. We must attempt to determine the intentions of the authors of the Constitution and whether or not the situation before us is, indeed, a *casus omissus*. We must also take into account the child's rights and establish what her wishes are with regard to the situation.'

He spoke for nearly forty more minutes about these issues. Mr Conolly looked at his watch and shook his head.

'At this rate,' he whispered, 'you won't get Evelyn today.'

The Chief Justice set a date in December for the judgment and added, 'Bring the child before this panel in chambers on Tuesday the twentieth day of December, 1955.'

A writ of *habeas corpus* was issued to the Minister in respect of 'the infant Evelyn Doyle'.

With that, the court was adjourned. Daddy was bitterly disappointed. He had hoped the case would be concluded that day. Mr Conolly met the press outside. Once again, he professed confidence in a victory, but said that, naturally, he was disappointed that the case would now drag on for another two months.

Granddad and Jessie didn't have to wait for Daddy to come home to hear the news; it was the lead story on the wireless. The Lord Mayor, Denis Larkin, was interviewed. He said that on behalf of Mr Doyle, he was disappointed that a decision had not been handed down, but added that he had every confidence in the court's mercy and justice. Jessie was devastated. She asked Granddad if there was any end in sight, and Granddad responded that there has to be an end to everything, one way or another. He quoted C S Lewis: 'The future is something that everyone reaches at the rate of sixty minutes an hour, whatever he does, whoever he is.'

When Daddy arrived home, Jessie and Granddad were surprised by his attitude; they had expected him to be utterly distraught. But he told them that after court had adjourned, Mr Conolly had advised him to follow up on the application for a Corporation house.

'TJ feels confident that the children will be home for Christmas,' he said. He explained to them about the writ of *habeas corpus*. 'According to TJ, the fact that the justices want to see Evelyn is a good sign.'

He said that he would go to the Housing Department in the Corporation offices tomorrow, and he asked Jessie to come with him.

The following day, Daddy and Jessie set out for the Housing Department, which was not far from Granddad's house. Gardiner Street was busy and, as they walked along, Daddy was stopped several times by strangers who recognized him from his pictures in the paper. They all wanted to shake his hand and wish him luck. Jessie teased him and said that he must feel like a film star.

'I wish I had as much money as a film star,' Daddy said. 'Then I wouldn't mind being recognized everywhere.'

With all the attention, Jessie was glad she had dressed carefully and put on powder and lipstick. She knew they made a handsome couple. As they strolled past Mountjoy Square, a couple of women approached for a chat. They told Daddy how sorry they were that he'd had to go through all this trouble.

Jessie spoke up. 'Well, that's all in the past. Now, we have to look forward.'

The older of the two women looked hard at Jessie. She'd picked up on her English accent. Blessing herself, she said, 'You'd be the Protestant housekeeper?'

Jessie didn't answer. The way the woman said 'house-keeper', she thought she might as well have said 'prostitute'.

Jessie felt sick; she wondered how she was going to survive in this country, with all its bitterness and prejudice. She tried to nudge Daddy along, but he had also caught the woman's innuendo and was not about to let the old biddie get away with it.

'Mind your own fecking business, you old bitch!' he said.

Jessie was a bit surprised but she knew that the strain of the past year was telling on Daddy.

'C'mon,' she said, 'let's go. I'm not bothered.'

But Daddy wanted to have his say.

'I don't suppose *you* would leave your home and country to look after someone else's children,' he hissed at the woman. 'No, I suppose not.'

The women blessed themselves and hurried away, more than a little shocked. Daddy told Jessie not to mind them.

'They're just fecking ignorant peasants.'

He took her hand, and they continued down Gardiner Street. It was just after ten o'clock when they reached the Corporation offices, which were located on the appropriately named Corporation Street. The waiting room was already packed with shabby women and screaming snotty-nosed children, just like it had been the first time Daddy was there. He put his handkerchief over his nose and mouth in a vain attempt to block out the stale odour. He and Jessie took a seat at the end of the last bench, inching along as the women in the queue were slowly attended to.

Out of nowhere, Daddy heard his name.

'It's him! It's Mr Doyle himself!'

The shriek had come from a woman who was dragging half a dozen kids behind her. Everyone in the room turned their heads and looked at Daddy and Jessie. A buzz of excited conversation went round the room. Daddy couldn't do anything but sit there as all the women and children stared at him. An official came through a door at the top of the room and approached Daddy.

Leaning forward, he whispered, 'Are you *the* Mr Doyle?'

'Well,' Daddy said, 'that would depend on which Mr Doyle you mean.'

The official said that he meant the Mr Desmond Doyle who'd been in all the papers.

Daddy admitted that he was that Mr Doyle. All the eyes in the room were still on him.

'Come with me, Mr Doyle,' the official said. 'And you too, Miss.'

He led Daddy and Jessie into a small private room and asked them to take a seat. Then he left the room. Daddy offered Jessie a cigarette and lit his own when she refused. A couple of minutes later, a short plump man came in. He was wearing a black suit with a gold watch chain attached to his waistcoat, and he carried a folder.

'I'm Mr O'Brien,' he said. 'I'm the Housing Manager. Very pleased to make your acquaintance. Now, let me see.'

He opened the folder, and Daddy saw the green form he had filled in all those months ago. Mr O'Brien read over the form, tapping his pen on the table as he went.

'Are your circumstances still the same as stated here, Mr Doyle?'

He passed the paper to Daddy, and Daddy scanned it and confirmed that things were still the same.

'You must be expecting big changes, though,' Mr O'Brien said. 'And sooner rather than later, I would think.'

Daddy wondered what the hell the old fool was on about.

'What do you mean?' he asked.

'Well, I thought maybe you would be needing a bigger house for when your children are released from those accursed schools. I spent twelve years in one myself,' he added.

Mr O'Brien told Daddy with pride, that he was able to exercise a certain amount of discretion in these matters and that, in view of Daddy's extraordinary circumstances, he would be able to offer him a house immediately.

'If you would just fill in the details here, we could get you sorted out.'

He handed Daddy a pink form. It was a formal offer of a 'dwelling'. Daddy completed the form, and Mr O'Brien took a set of keys from his jacket pocket. They were keys to a house. Daddy was overwhelmed with gratitude and shook the man's hand. Mr O'Brien showed them out and, when Daddy and Jessie were alone on the street, Daddy looked at the tag attached to the keys to see where the house was.

'It says 62 Kildonan Drive, Finglas West.'

They hurried back to Granddad's to tell him the good news, and Daddy invited Granddad to go with them to see the house. Less than an hour later, Daddy put the key in the lock on the blue door. He was thrilled to find that Mr O'Brien had given them a brand-new three-bedroom house with gardens at both the front and back.

'And guess what,' he said, 'I didn't even have to write to the Taoiseach to get it.'

Daddy and Granddad went round measuring the floors

for lino and estimating how much paint they would need. Occasionally, they asked Jessie for her opinion on the colours and a good-natured argument would follow. Jessie imagined the wonders of a bright new bathroom and the luxury of a good soak in private, and she marvelled at the modern kitchen, with its door that opened straight onto the garden.

The next time Daddy and Jessie came to visit me, they took me to see the new house. Granddad was there, painting the living room. Daddy told me that as I was a big girl now, I would have the small bedroom all to myself, and he let me pick the colour for the walls. He said I could choose between cream, pale cream or off-white. I picked the pale cream. It seemed unbelievable that, at last, we were all going to be together again. I asked Daddy if we would be home for Christmas.

'I think so, pet,' he said, 'but we mustn't count our chickens just yet.'

He started to paint alongside Granddad and told me to go help Jessie. She was in the bathroom, polishing the huge copper hot water tank till it shone. Although I had made up my mind to 'get on' with Jessie, I still avoided being with her whenever I could. Instead of helping her, I made a nuisance of myself where Daddy and Granddad were working. They worried that I would get paint on my clothes.

'Go and see what your mammy is doing,' Daddy said.

Even though Daddy had referred to Jessie as my 'mammy' many times before, now that we were in the new house, I was shocked to hear the word. It brought home to me the reality of the future and the changes that were in store. Now I would actually have to live with the new mammy and it felt all wrong. In the back of my mind, a little bit of fear formed at the prospect.

When Daddy dropped me off at the convent later that day, I told him, 'I don't want to go to that house with *her* there.'

Daddy said that surely I didn't mean that. Hadn't I been getting on all right with the new mammy?

'Why have you changed your mind?' he asked. 'Has someone said something to you? You must be tired, pet. I promise everything will be all right when the boys are home and we're all together again. You must try and like your new mammy.'

I wished he would stop calling her 'my mammy'. It seemed that every time he said it, I grew more certain that I could never like her. I told Siobhán about it, and she said that she wouldn't care if she had a new mammy or not.

'I just wish my daddy would come for me,' she said. 'Consider yourself lucky.'

Mother Paul told me that I wouldn't be singing the solo in the concert that Christmas.

'You probably won't be with us this year, dear.'

I was very disappointed because I had been practising for a good few weeks. I had an empty, fluttery feeling in my stomach, and I couldn't understand what that was all about.

I asked Mother Bernadette, and she said I was probably worrying about the great changes that would take place when I left the convent.

'And after all,' she said, 'the outcome of the case still

isn't certain. Nobody knows what the judges will rule. It's a very serious decision they have to make.' She said that although the judges were very wise men, they still needed the help and guidance of Our Lord, and she told me that we must pray that they would make the right decision.

Daddy didn't take me to the new house again. He would visit me for a short time on Saturdays and Sundays on his way to Finglas. I wasn't worried about not seeing the house, as long as I didn't have to see Jessie. When Granny's parcel of tea and green ribbons had arrived the previous week, Granny'd said in her letter that my real mammy 'had been asking after you and saying prayers for you'. Her words made me cry. That was the last letter I received from Granny, though I still got her packages.

The nuns were getting the convent ready for Christmas. Apart from Mother Paul, who said I wouldn't be singing in the concert, and Mother Teresa, who didn't give me new wool to make winter mittens, no one excluded me from anything. I was still to be included in the Nativity Play, and I made parcels for 'the black babies' in Africa, alongside the other girls. But in a funny way, I felt left out, as though I was already gone. The nuns were as kind to me as ever, but something had changed. Sometimes, I thought I might like to stay in the convent and not go home at all. Or, I thought, I'd like to go back to the flats and my friends there. The flats were familiar and safe while the new house seemed lonely and cold. I tried not to think about it too much but I didn't always succeed.

When Mother Imelda saw me brooding, she would say, 'All those frown lines will stay forever, dear, and you won't be pretty any more.'

*

Daddy told Mr Conolly and Nick that he was worried about the justices interviewing me. He wasn't sure what I would tell them. Despite the nice things I'd said to Mr Conolly about Jessie, I now seemed determined to dislike her.

Mr Conolly said that he would have another talk with me. But in any case, he added, they still hoped that the judges' decision would be based on the argument that the Children Act was repugnant to the Constitution rather than on anything I might say.

'To tell you the truth, Desmond, not too many land-mark decisions come out of that Court. But if I were a betting man, I would give you odds of 3/2 in our favour. *Nil desperandum*, as they say. Despair at nothing. We'll work on the little sweet together.'

A couple of weeks before Christmas, Daddy took me to see Mr Conolly. On the way to his office, we stopped in the city centre because Daddy wanted to buy some presents. He left the car at St Stephen's Green, and we walked down Grafton Street. All the shops were bright and gay with Christmas decorations and coloured fairy lights. I saw two or three Santies, and Daddy explained that they were the 'real' Santy's helpers. I didn't tell him that I knew Santy wasn't real, that he was just for little ones like my baby brothers. An old raggy man was playing jigs and reels on a tin whistle, and people were throwing pennies in an Oxo tin in front of him. Every time someone threw a coin in, he would stop playing and say, 'God bless ye'. When he saw me watching him, the old man smiled and winked at me. He had sparkly blue eyes, and I smiled back at him.

There were tinker women on the street too. They had their babies wrapped in shawls tied on their backs. As they moved through the crowds, they begged for 'a few coppers for the children'. Most people ignored them. They looked so dirty, I wished someone would give them some pennies to buy soap. Daddy told me not to mind them. He said that, more than likely, they had more money than he did. When we got to O'Connell Street, we saw a brass band playing Christmas carols outside Clery's. I was sad when I heard them, and I felt the lump in my chest for the first time in ages. Daddy led me into Clery's. I thought we were going to the toy department but instead we went up the wide wooden stairs to the department that sold women's clothes. He put me on a chair and told me to wait there for him. I could see him talking to a pretty saleslady. She showed him some women's coats. After he'd looked at lots of coats, he chose a beige one with a fur collar. I knew it was for Jessie, and it put me in bad humour. Daddy brought the coat over to where I was sitting and held it up.

'What do you think of that, Ebbs, pet? Will your mammy like it?'

I said, 'I'm sure *she* will like it, but *I* wouldn't be caught dead in it.'

I could see that I had hurt Daddy's feelings and I felt bad, but I just looked away from him and the coat. Poor Daddy. He didn't know what to do. He was hoping that Mr Conolly would be able to turn my attitude around.

We went down to the men's department, and Daddy let me choose a present for Granddad. I picked a box of monogrammed hankies with G's on them, but Daddy said that Granddad's name began with H, so I swapped them. Then I asked the man behind the counter for some socks. I told him that I had to make sure the socks were long enough to wrap all the way around Granddad's head and I asked him if he could stretch them for me. Daddy laughed, and the man laughed too and shook his head. I didn't know what was so funny. Didn't everyone's Granddad get headaches?

I handed over the ten shilling note that Daddy had given me to buy the presents and the man gave me one shilling and a penny change. Daddy told me to hold onto the change so that I could buy some sweets to share with my friends at the convent. Then he took me to Woolworth's to see the fairy grotto. Afterwards, we had dinner in the restaurant and, for a treat, I got a new American sweet called a knickerbocker glory. It had coloured layers of jelly in it, and cream and fruit and ice cream. On top, there was a cherry. Daddy watched in disbelief as I finished every last spoonful. I spent ages choosing sweets to take back to the girls. By that time, we were nearly late to see Mr Conolly. We hurried back towards St Stephen's Green as fast as we could, laughing as we went. Daddy pretended to be a car, saying 'beeb-beeb' when anyone got in our way. When we reached the busy street, he picked me up and ran across. I squealed, and all the people passing by smiled at us.

Mr Conolly was waiting at his office.

This time he didn't shake my hand, but hugged me instead and said, 'Ah, it's my favourite little sweet.'

He and Daddy talked for a few minutes about 'the judgment' and the possibility of it not going in our favour.

Then Mr Conolly turned to me and said, 'Well, my sweet, it might all be down to you. Can you help us?'

He explained that in a few days' time, Daddy was going to take me to the court where some nice gentlemen would ask me a lot of questions. He said that he was going to help me by telling me what to say.

'Now you're not to be frightened, you see, because your daddy will be sitting close by and you'll be able to see him when you're talking to the men. Do you understand?'

I told him that I wasn't frightened of anything, as long as Daddy was there.

'Good. Now, what about Mrs Brown?'

I said that I didn't know anyone named Mrs Brown, and Mr Conolly explained that she was the lady who was going to be my new mammy.

'Of course,' he said, 'we all know that she is not really your mammy, but we have to pretend, don't we?'

I told him that so long as she wasn't *really* a new mammy, it was all right.

'Evelyn,' Mr Conolly said, 'the gentlemen I mentioned are going to ask you who you would rather live with, your real mammy, who has gone away, or your daddy. Do you want to tell me what you would say to that?'

I thought about it for a minute. I wanted to live with Daddy and my brothers, but that would mean living with my pretend mammy too. As for my real mammy, I didn't even know where she was, so how could I choose her? Daddy was watching me, and I knew that when I made my decision, I could never go back on it. I didn't want to say anything. I started to cry and Mr Conolly told Daddy that it might be better to leave it for today. I felt miserable. I thought I was letting Daddy and Mr Conolly down, but I was confused and unhappy.

Daddy said, 'Don't worry, pet. Everything will be all right.' Then he told Mr Conolly that it was an awful lot to put on a child's shoulders. 'Find another way to win.'

He sounded annoyed. Mr Conolly said he would talk it over with Nick.

At the convent, Mother Bernadette helped me to wrap up Granddad's Christmas gifts.

'You're very quiet, child,' she said. 'Is something worrying you?'

I described my visit to Mr Conolly's office and said that I had to go to court the following week to talk to the justices.

'I'm not afraid of the men,' I said, 'but I don't know what to answer them about the new mammy.'

She told me that we all had to make decisions throughout our lives.

'And sometimes,' she said, 'we have to make very big and important ones that will deeply affect other people, in which case, we can't think only of ourselves.' She assured me that if I asked Him, God would help me.

I had a nightmare that night. Jessie had all my brothers wrapped in a big black cloak with a red lining. Daddy was under the water in the Liffey again and Mammy was waving goodbye to us all. I was alone with a snarling Rex.

The day I had to go and see the justices, Mother Teresa got me ready. She fixed my hair and tied a new green ribbon in a bow on top of my head. We were in the sewing room for over an hour as she put first one dress, then another on me. Finally, she decided on the first outfit she had tried.

'Better to have you in your school uniform, dear.'

She dressed me in a dark green gymslip, yellow shirt and emerald-green tie. This was the first time I had worn the big girls' uniform, and I was thrilled. She gave me a pair of patent leather shoes that fastened with a strap across the top of my foot and buttoned on the side. They were the most beautiful shoes I had ever seen. When we were all finished, she took me to Reverend Mother's office.

'Sit down child,' the Reverend Mother said. 'We must have a little chat before your father comes for you.'

This was the first time I had been alone with the Reverend Mother, and I was nervous. She smiled at me.

'How have you liked being here with us? That is a question you will be asked today, my dear, and you must be truthful.'

I noticed that she had forgotten my name again.

'I want you to know,' she continued, 'that whatever you say, and no matter what the court's decision is on Wednesday, we love you, and our prayers are with you.'

This was very serious stuff. Me, in the Reverend Mother's prayers! Holy Mother of God.

'You are being taken to see the justices so they can have a little chat with you before they make up their minds about whether to send you home with your daddy. Evelyn, my dear, you do want to go with your daddy, don't you?'

When she called me by my name, I got a warm feeling inside my chest; I smiled at her. The convent had become my home and I felt safe and secure there. Nothing bad had happened to me since I'd come to live there, apart from wondering if the devil would visit the dormitory if I slept on my stomach. I was confused. I desperately wanted to be with Daddy and my brothers, but the house in Finglas felt strange to me, and I had no idea what our new life would be like. I wondered why what I said to the justices was going to be so important; normally, grown-ups didn't bother about what children thought. I told the Reverend Mother that I had been very happy at the convent. I said that if I had to leave, I would miss all my friends and the Mothers. She told me that I would soon get used to family life again.

'You will always be welcome to visit us,' she said. 'But let's see what happens first, shall we? Then we can talk about the future.'

Mother Bernadette knocked on the door and said that Daddy was downstairs waiting for me. The Reverend Mother bent down and hugged me, and I nearly fainted with fright. She had never done that before. She smelled of freshly washed clothes and violets. A few wispy white hairs were sticking out of her chin. I couldn't wait to tell the other girls that the Reverend Mother had hugged me. She went back to her desk and took something out of a drawer.

'This is for you, child. It will help you to be strong and to know that Our Lady is always with you.'

She put a white leather purse in my hand and blessed me. Written on the purse in gold letters were the words of the Hail Mary, and inside was the prettiest rosary I had ever seen. It had a gold chain and crucifix, and the beads looked like tiny pearls. I got a big lump in my throat. I thought I was going to cry. It was the nicest thing anyone had ever given me, nicer even than Molly.

Daddy seemed jumpy as we drove towards the city. He was swearing at the other cars, and he shouted out of the window at a bus driver, 'Did you get your feckin driving licence out of a lucky bag? You bloody gobshite!'

Even my new rosary wouldn't save Daddy from purgatory. I asked him why he was so annoyed with everyone today.

'Are you annoyed with me too?' I said.

'No pet, I'm not. I'm under a lot of strain, waiting for the decision on our case.'

He said not to mind him. He told me he'd be his old self again soon.

The traffic was heavy all the way into town and, when the rain started lashing down, we had to go even slower, which didn't improve Daddy's mood. I felt sorry for the poor horses, who had their heads turned down against the wind and rain. They had to pull carts through the traffic on the slippy roads and try to keep out of the way of buses and trams. Finally, we parked close to the Four Courts and dashed through the rain. There were people sheltering near the entrance, and Daddy pushed through them and found an usher, who told us to have a seat. While we waited, a few men came over to Daddy and chatted to him about 'his brave fight'. One of them said it was time someone had the courage to 'take on the bastards'. Another put a sixpence in my hand and blessed me.

The usher came back and told us to follow him. He led us down a long corridor. We passed several men in black gowns, still wearing the wigs they wore in court. Finally, we reached a huge door. The usher knocked, and we waited until we heard someone call, 'Enter.'

The justices' chambers seemed enormous and contained the longest table I had ever seen. I tried to count the chairs around it, but there were too many. Three old men in pin-stripe suits were sitting in leather chairs, drinking tea from little white and gold cups.

'Your Honours,' the usher said, 'Mr Doyle and Miss Doyle.'

I felt very grand being called 'Miss Doyle'. One of the men came over and asked me if it was all right to call me 'Evelyn'.

'That will be all right, Mister,' I said.

Then he told the usher to take Daddy to the tea room. Daddy said he wanted to stay.

'Evelyn might be a bit frightened on her own.'

The man said that I would be perfectly all right. Turning to me, he asked, 'Won't you, my dear?'

I liked this old man. He reminded me of the Santy in one of my storybooks, except his white beard was shorter and he had sparkly eyes that seemed to smile all by them-selves. I told Daddy that I would be all right and that he was not to worry about me. After Daddy left the room, the old man with the beard took my hand and led me over to where the others were sitting. He motioned for me to sit down on a little leather stool.

The other two gentlemen said, 'Hello.'

They told me that there was nothing to worry about, they just wanted to have a little chat with me. A man with dark hair gave me a glass of lemonade. They asked me to begin by telling them all about myself. A third man started writing on a big yellow pad and the man who reminded me of Santy was looking at me and asking questions about the convent. I told him that I liked feeding the pigs but didn't like the cows. I also said that I'd cut my hair myself and that I'd never had ringworm.

'Daddy would go mad if I had no hair at all,' I said.

They laughed at this and I was glad that I was making them happy. The man who was writing asked me to tell them about 'the lady' who was going to look after us if I went home to live with Daddy.

'You mean the new mammy?' I asked.

He nodded and said, 'What is she like?'

I wasn't sure what they wanted me to say. I remembered that the Reverend Mother had told me to tell the truth.

'Well,' I began, 'she's English and she makes Daddy laugh, and my real mammy didn't make him laugh. My real mammy isn't ever coming back, you know. Mr Conolly asked me if I wanted to live with her, but I don't know where she is. Daddy says she is in a place called "shagging Scotland", though.'

The man who was writing turned his back to me and the other two men started coughing into their hankies until their faces turned red. When they looked at me again, their eyes were watery, and they wiped at them with their hankies.

'Would you like to go home and live with your daddy and your brothers?' the dark-haired man asked.

I told him that I would love to go home and live with my daddy and my brothers. But I said I didn't think it would be the same since Mammy wasn't there anymore.

'Do you not want to live with your new mammy?'

I didn't think I needed a new mammy, but I knew that if I said that I would be letting Daddy and Mr Conolly down. I clamped my hands between my knees and hunched my shoulders forward, trying to think of what to say. The man who looked like Santy told me to take my time. He said I should tell them whatever I wanted.

'Forget what anyone has said to you, my dear. Just tell us how *you* feel.'

I made up my mind.

'I want my real mammy to come home, but I know she's not able to. So I suppose I must have the new mammy. Then Daddy will be happy and the boys won't have to go to the Christian Brothers.'

Mother Bernadette had said that sometimes we have to think of others, 'as the Lord did', and not only ourselves. The man asked me if I was sure that this was what I wanted. He said that I could change my mind if I liked.

'No,' I said, 'I want to go home with Daddy, and I'm sure my brothers want to come home as well.'

When the men were finished with their questions, the usher took me back to where Daddy was waiting. Daddy asked me what had happened in the chambers and I told him that I couldn't remember everything we said.

'But I know I told them that I wanted to go home with you.'

He said I was a good girl and that Mammy would be pleased. We went back to Granddad's house, and Jessie made our tea. Daddy tried all through the meal to get me to talk to Jessie.

'Tell your mammy about your friends at the convent,' he

said. And, 'Tell your mammy about the time we went to the Phoenix Park and you carried the camera for me. Do you remember that day? There was just you and me and Noel.'

I let him tell the stories, and I said as little as I could get away with. Granddad didn't say much either and, after we'd finished our tea, he asked me if I would go to the shops with him to buy cigarettes.

'And some Pontefract cakes, if you're lucky.'

Daddy said that I should help Mammy with the washing up, but Granddad said there was hardly any washing up to do and surely she could manage it herself.

Granddad and I walked hand in hand down Innisfallen Parade and out onto Dorset Street. It was raining, but we didn't mind. Granddad had his trilby hat on and he pulled the collar of his coat up to his ears. I pulled the hood of my cloak over my head. He asked me if there was anything I'd like to talk to him about.

'You can say whatever you want. So, darling, if something is worrying you, tell me about it.'

I trusted Granddad as much as I trusted Daddy. He had been my pal ever since I could remember. I told him that I wasn't looking forward to having Jessie for a mammy.

'I told the nice men at the court that I wanted to go home and live with Daddy and the boys, but...'

I couldn't explain how I really felt, but Granddad was a step ahead of me.

'But you're not sure about Mrs Brown? You want your mammy to come back so you can all live happily ever after, I suppose?'

I said that that was exactly what I wanted and didn't

understand why things couldn't be like that.

'Well, my dear sweet child, I am an old man now and I have found to be true something a great poet said long ago. "The secret of life is not to do what one likes, but to try to like that which one has to do." Do you understand? You did what was necessary today and now you must live with that in the best way you can.'

I knew what Granddad meant and I thought that, as long as I had Daddy and my brothers, it mightn't be so bad. Granddad was very old and wise, and I believed whatever he told me. Whenever I asked him how old he was, he said a hundred and four.

'Besides,' he said, 'I will look out for you. Come on, we'd better buy some sweets and get you back to the convent before the nuns send out search parties.'

When Daddy left me at the convent that evening, he said, 'I hope this will be the last time we ever say goodnight on this doorstep, pet. This time tomorrow you might be at home for good with Mammy and me.'

He kissed me goodbye, and I watched him drive away. Mother Imelda brought me in off the doorstep, and I held her hand tightly as we walked along the corridor with all the saints looking down on us. I couldn't understand why I felt such a huge sadness and why I couldn't seem to get excited about the prospect of this being my last night in the convent. I stood for a moment at the dormitory door and watched my friends running around in their long white nightgowns, doing all the usual night-time things: emptying the wash basins, brushing each other's hair, laughing at their secret jokes. A new girl was being helped by an older one, just as I had been, and a group of three or four other girls were sitting on a bed in the far corner, practising their lines for the Christmas play. I felt as though I wasn't a part of the convent any more, and the girls seemed barely to notice me as I came into the dormitory. I got ready for bed as quickly and quietly as possible and hid under the blankets until Mother Imelda said prayers and switched out the lights.

EIGHT

Daddy was up early the next morning and left the house without waking Jessie or Granddad. He drove to Church Street and parked the car. He needed to be alone to think, and he decided to walk for a while. The bustle of daily life hadn't started yet and the streets were still quiet. The only sounds, apart from his own footsteps, were the odd milk cart, pulled by half knackered horses, the lads whistling as they delivered the morning papers, and the dowdy old biddies trudging home after cleaning the offices and shops.

When Daddy reached the Four Courts, he stopped and stood looking at it for several minutes. There were still scars on the portico pillars from when the building had been occupied by anti-treaty forces during the Civil War in 1922. Now, he thought, his own battle would end here, one way or another. Today, he might finally get his family back. He walked all the way down Ormond Quay and across O'Connell Street and down as far as the Custom House, once a centre of the British administration before Ireland won its independence. It had been almost totally destroyed by fire in 1921, but had not been restored yet. Daddy found a greasy little café in Amiens Street where the dock workers had their early morning mugs of tea and big farls of hot soda bread, slathered thick with melting butter. He ordered a mug of tea, chose a corner, and attempted to be invisible. He knew he looked out of place among the working men, with his suit and polished shoes. As he drank his tea, he wondered how he was going to feel a few hours from now, when he finally heard the judges' decision.

When the hands on the grimy clock were nearing ten, Daddy thought he'd better head back towards the Four Courts. As he reached Upper Ormond Quay, he could see a crowd of newspapermen and photographers gathered outside. He pulled the collar of his coat up as far as it would go and tugged the brim of his trilby down, trying to look inconspicuous. To his relief, he strolled past the crowd unnoticed. Granddad was sitting alone on a bench in the furthest corner of the foyer, smoking a cigarette and reading the *Irish Independent*. There was a stillness about him that gave Daddy confidence. As Daddy approached, he saw the headline on the front page of Granddad's newspaper: SUPREME COURT DECISION TODAY IN CUSTODY BATTLE. Daddy sat beside him, and Granddad put his paper down.

'Thank you for coming,' Daddy said.

'Of course I came. What are fathers for? Whichever way it goes, and I pray to God it goes your way, son, you need your family with you. And God help you, I'm all you've got.'

Mr Conolly spotted them and hurried over. He shook hands with Granddad and Daddy, then told them it was time to go in.

'Nick should be in there already, and I expect Michael wouldn't miss it for the world.'

Granddad took a seat inside the court on one of the press benches, and Daddy sat at the barristers' table at the front of the room. Nick and Mr Beatty were there, looking over some papers.

Daddy asked the barristers what they thought the chances of winning were.

'It all depends on how they viewed Evelyn's constitutional rights and Section 10 of the Children Act,' Mr Conolly said. 'We'll know soon enough.'

Daddy said that when the justices had interviewed me the day before, I'd told them that I wanted to come home, and he felt sure I'd said nothing to discourage them from ruling in our favour. The Minister's barristers arrived and nodded at Daddy's team. Mr Conolly went over to their table and shook hands with Mr Kenny and the others.

'Well, gentlemen,' he said, his voice booming around the courtroom, 'it's been a mostly fair fight and may the best man win.'

An usher called for silence and told everyone to be upstanding. The buzz of conversation died. The five justices filed in. Daddy's heart was in his mouth as Justice Kingsmill-Moore began to speak. He read over Section 10 of the Children Act.

Then he said, 'Not withstanding the question of whether that section is repugnant to the constitution, this court must take cognisance of the child Evelyn Doyle's right to choose as provided for in Article 42, Subsection 5 of the Constitution.'

Daddy and his barristers had their heads down, not daring to look at the bench. Mr Conolly gripped a pencil so tightly that it snapped in half. They listened as the justice related parts of the interview conducted with me the day before.

'However, while it was determined that the child is intelligent and articulate, this Bench has concluded that the wishes expressed by the child were influenced by other parties and may not necessarily be an accurate reflection of her desires. Therefore, however reluctantly, we cannot take her stated wishes into consideration.'

When Justice Kingsmill-Moore had finished, the Chief Justice began. He addressed the court for over an hour about a number of issues involved in the case. He spoke of Daddy's willingness to 'resume control' of my education and the question of whether the State had the authority to interfere with that right. He praised Daddy for having secured permanent employment and having obtained a house that was adequate to his family's needs. He also pointed out the seriousness of declaring invalid any statute that contained provisions which, if they stood alone, would be quite in accord with the Constitution.

By now, it was nearly lunch-time, and the justices seemed to Daddy no nearer to announcing their decision. What he'd heard so far didn't sound promising, and he'd grown more and more dejected as the morning wore on. He wanted to get everything over with but, at the same time, if the justices were going to rule against him, he certainly wasn't eager to hear it. The next thing he knew, the Chief Justice was adjourning for lunch and ordering all parties to reconvene at two thirty. An usher called for everyone to be upstanding. Daddy and his team remained, while the court was being cleared. Mr Conolly asked if anyone wanted lunch. Nick and Mr Beatty said they would nip out for a quick sandwich.

'What about you, Desmond?' Mr Beatty asked.

Daddy said that he wasn't hungry and told them to go ahead. He wanted to be alone for a while.

Mr Conolly patted Daddy's shoulder as he left the table and said, 'It's still not clear what their decision is. Don't give up.'

Daddy sensed Granddad beside him before he saw him. Granddad sat down. Daddy had his head in his hands. When he felt Granddad's hand on his shoulder, he couldn't contain himself and the tears came. Granddad said nothing for a while; it was as well for Daddy to let the tension out. Although it was completely out of character, Granddad put his arms around Daddy.

The court was empty now but for them, and the usher was waiting. Daddy blew his nose and wiped his eyes.

'Christ, Dad, I need a drink,' he said.

Granddad told him to go and splash some cold water on his face but Daddy said, 'Come on, let's just go.'

'You're assuming you've lost,' Granddad said. '*Fiat justitia et ruant coeli.*'

'What does that mean?'

'Roughly, it means justice will be done, though the heavens fall. I know justice will be done today. Have courage, son.'

The usher let them out a side door and told them to knock when they came back. Daddy was grateful for this kindness. He didn't feel able to face the relentless questions of the press just then. Granddad bought him a large brandy and persuaded him to eat a sandwich. Mr Conolly and Nick and Mr Beatty found them and sat down. They were all in a sombre mood, but Mr Conolly said that whatever the outcome of the case was, they were all going to have dinner at the Gresham Hotel that night.

'And it's on me,' he said.

Daddy told him that he didn't think he'd be in any mood for socializing.

'Where do we go from here?' he asked.

'Straight to High Park, we hope,' Nick replied.

They made their way back to court. When the usher called for all to be upstanding, a shuffling noise filled the great room. People had their last minute coughs and cleared their throats. Daddy tried to read the justices' faces as they filed into the room, but the men gave nothing away.

Justice O'Dálaigh spoke briefly, addressing the argument put forth by the Minister's counsel that Article 42 did not apply in the case of broken families.

'...desertion on the part of a mother without just cause leaves the authority of the family unimpaired and in no way diminishes the parental right with regard to the education of the children.'

Justice O'Dálaigh sat down. The Chief Justice cleared his throat, preparing to speak.

'In the view of this Court,' he began, 'Subsection 5 of Article 42 does not enable the legislature to take away the right of a parent who is in a position to do so to control the education of his child, where there is nothing culpable on the part of either parent or child.'

Daddy looked at Mr Conolly, but Mr Conolly gave no sign; he was listening intently to the Chief Justice.

'The Court doth, in answer to the question submitted to it for determination in the said case stated, declare that Section 10 of the Children Act is invalid as being repugnant to the Constitution, in as much and insofar as it deprives a parent with whose consent a child has been sent to a certified industrial school of the right to resume control of that child so as to provide for its education when that parent is willing and able to do so.'

The public gallery erupted with cheers and shouts. Daddy sat stunned for a minute. Then he slumped in his seat, unable to hold back tears of joy. Mr Conolly was pumping Daddy's hand, and Daddy heard him saying, 'We've won! We've won!'

After several minutes, order was restored in the courtroom. By then, nearly all the pressmen had left, and most of the public had gathered outside in the foyer and on the steps to wait for Daddy to come out. He hardly heard the rest of the judgment, he was shaking so badly.

'And it is ordered and adjudged that the said parties showing cause do pay to the said Desmond Doyle his costs of the case stated...'

The only people left in court to obey the instruction to be upstanding were the Minister's barristers and Daddy's team, who all bowed to the justices as they rose and disappeared through the little side door near the end of the bench.

As Daddy walked out of the court, he could see an enormous crowd spilling out of the vast foyer of the building and onto the steps. He asked Mr Conolly to sneak him out the side door.

'Let them have their hero for a few minutes, Desmond,' Mr Conolly said. 'It's like the man said, you are David who slew Goliath, and they supported you every step of the way. Go out there and let them share in your victory. That's all they want.'

Nick and Mr Beatty stood behind Daddy, and Mr Conolly gave him a little nudge out into the foyer. A great cheer went up from the crowd and it seemed to Daddy as though a hundred flashbulbs went off. Lots of men were clapping him on the back as he made his way towards the main door, and he didn't know which way to turn. In the confusion, he couldn't see Granddad anywhere. A sleek black Rolls Royce pulled up in front of the Four Courts and the Lord Mayor, complete with his chain of office, got out of the back seat. The crowd parted as Denis Larkin made his way towards Daddy.

'Congratulations, Mr Doyle!' he said, smiling at the cameras. 'My car is at your disposal. Shall we go and collect your daughter now?'

Mother Bernadette had tears in her eyes.

'Your Daddy has won his case, darling, and you're going home today. My, but we're going to miss you.'

She walked with me to the dormitory and helped me pack my few personal possessions into a small brown case. Mother Imelda appeared. She made no attempt to hide the fact that she was crying. She sniffed loudly as she went about her chores in the bathroom. Six or seven of my best friends came in and sat on Siobhán's bed, watching silently as I prepared to leave. A sadness hung over the room and, for once, the girls were not scolded by Mother Bernadette for being in the dormitory during the day. We heard the front doorbell in the distance, and Siobhán ran to the window.

'They're here!' she called.

Mother Bernadette hugged me tightly and told me that I

would always be in her thoughts and prayers. Mother Imelda said that she was too busy to come downstairs with me.

'So I'll say goodbye here. Be a good girl, now.' She hugged me and winked as she said, 'I should have got you to teach me how to do that knot in the bootlaces. Goodbye, darling. I'll miss you.'

I ran from the dormitory and raced down the stairs, leaving my opened case behind me on the bed. I was trying to be happy that Daddy had won, but these goodbyes were making me very sad. The Reverend Mother was waiting at the bottom of the staircase. She took my hand and led me along the hallway to the front door.

'These doors will always be open for you, child. You will be greatly missed. Remember us in your prayers.'

She made the sign of the cross on my forehead and kissed my cheek before opening the door. The driveway was full of motorcars. Daddy jumped out of an enormous black one, and the Lord Mayor followed behind him. I ran to Daddy, and he lifted me up and twirled me around.

'You're coming home for good today, pet. Are you happy?'

I said I was happy, though I didn't know if I was or not. The men from the press took dozens of photographs, and Daddy told them that he was thrilled to bits with the judgment. Denis Larkin said that he knew all along Daddy would win. Daddy told me that we were all going to a party at the Gresham Hotel and that Mr Conolly would be there with Mr Beatty and Nick. As we climbed into the big car, I saw a lot of the girls standing at the door of the convent, waving goodbye, but Siobhán wasn't among them.

Mother Bernadette was walking over to the car with my suitcase, and little Ann McCafferty ran past her, clutching Molly.

'You forgot her,' she said, holding out the doll to me.

I said no, that I hadn't forgotten.

'She lives here,' I told her. 'She wouldn't want to leave. But just don't put her in the basin with her head under the water.'

I looked up and saw Siobhán at the dormitory window. I waved to her. I knew that she was crying, as she waved goodbye to me, watching me head off into the future. It would be a happy one, wouldn't it? As I climbed into the big motorcar I clutched my rosary tightly and asked Our Lady to leave the convent with me.

THE END